GOOD
HOUSEKEEPING

One Pot Magic

COOKING WITH YOUR AIR FRYER,
CASSEROLE DISH, DUTCH OVEN, PRESSURE COOKER,
SHEET PAN & SLOW COOKER

HEARST
HOME

Contents

Introduction

:::::::::::::::::::::::::

While it can be enjoyable to cook satisfying recipes that require multiple steps and just as many pans, let's face it: on most weeknights the goal is to serve up a delicious dinner that's quick and easy. All of the dinners found in this book are one-pot recipes—those that require little more than a knife, cutting board, mixing bowls and your pot or appliance of choice.

Within these pages you'll find more than 180 recipes—all developed, tested and approved by Good Housekeeping's Test Kitchen editors. These satisfying, all-in-one meals come together in a snap and require minimal cleanup too. You choose the method, and we'll help you get dinner on the table, whether you're using a Dutch oven, sheet pan or casserole dish, skillet, air fryer, Instant Pot or slow cooker. Yes, they're all here!

Each chapter begins with a thorough introduction with everything you need to know to master the techniques and make the best use of the appliance or pan, beginning with an overview of the method and the cooking applications it does best, care recommendations, cooking cheat sheets and top Good Housekeeping Test Kitchen tips for success. And in case you're looking to buy any of the appliances or pots used to make these recipes, the Good Housekeeping Institute shares their choice for Best All-Around model and its favorite features, plus insight into their product testing process. Need more info? Simply scan the QR code in the chapter introduction for a deeper dive into features and reviews of other top picks. We'll also help you equip your kitchen to efficiently tackle any of these recipes with ease. Turn the page and let's get started!

QUICK GUIDE

Looking for a recipe that comes together quickly or is guaranteed to be a hit with the family? We've added labels throughout the book to make it easy for you to spot the following:

≡ VEGETARIAN ≡
Make it meatless! You won't find fish, chicken, pork or beef here.

≡ VEGAN ≡
And these recipes have no dairy and eggs either.

≡ QUICK & EASY ≡
Short on time? These recipes take 30 minutes or less from start to finish.

≡ FAMILY FRIENDLY ≡
These comfort food recipes go easy on spice and are sure to please everyone, including little ones.

Chapter 1

Getting Started

Ready to get cooking? Not so fast. All of the one-pot recipes on these pages will come together seamlessly if you begin by equipping your kitchen with a few quality tools, plus keep a well-stocked pantry and keep a few tips in your back pocket.

First things, first: Each of the chapters focuses on a specific one-pot method. Here's a quick play-by-play of the appliances and cookware needed to make the recipes. For more details about the strengths of each method, tips for getting the best results and reviews of current models, turn to the specific chapter.

Dutch Oven
This sturdy pot is ideal for browning or braising roasts and stews on the stovetop as well as in the oven. A 5½- to 7-quart Dutch oven is the most useful, but they also come in 4½-quart and smaller sizes. The versatile Dutch oven is perfect for making anything from Chicken Mole (page 37) to White Wine Mussels (page 43).

Sheet Pan
While a baking sheet might bring cookies to mind, they are also fantastic for throwing together a quick and easy weeknight meal. Try the Slow Roasted Lamb with Pistachio Gremolata (page 85) and the Garam Masala Roasted Chicken and Cauliflower (page 55), dinners with maximum flavor and minimum cleanup. Choose heavy, metal baking sheets that can withstand high temperatures. For roasting vegetables, we suggest a rimmed baking sheet. We recommend using 18 x 13-inch baking sheets, which are the standard for a half-sheet.

Casserole Dish
For bakeware that you can pull straight from the oven and place on the table, look no further than the versatile casserole dish. Bake a Classic Lasagna (page 83); Ham, Cheddar, and Red Onion Bread Pudding (page 93); or a Tex-Mex Tortilla Casserole (page 77) to perfection in a casserole dish. Choose oval or rectangular dishes with sides about 2 inches high; 10 x 15 inches (4 quarts), 13 x 9 inches (3½ quarts), 11 x 7 inches (6 cups), and 8 inches square (1½ quarts) are the most common. Depending on the model, casseroles can be ceramic, glass or even cast iron, and may come with a snap-on cover for easy transport and storage.

Skillet

So many meals can be made in the simple skillet! Think Skillet Mac & Cheese (page 127), Chicken Paprikash (page 117) or Spicy Shakshuka (page 111). Opt for a small (7- to 8-inch) one for omelets and other single-serve dishes and a large (12-inch) one as your weeknight workhorse. Choose a pan that can be used both on the stovetop and in the oven.

Air Fryer

Air fryers have heating elements that act like a broiler and large fans to circulate heat, resulting in extra crispy food that's prepared with less oil. They typically heat up very quickly and bake or roast food quickly and evenly, thanks to the combination of a concentrated heat source and the size and placement of the fan. Make delectable Crab Cakes with Gingery Slaw (page 151), Buttermilk Fried Chicken (page 159) and Fast Steak Frites (page 165).

Instant Pot

This versatile device combines the benefits of multiple kitchen appliances in one space-saving kitchen machine. With a press of a button, the Instant Pot simplifies everyday cooking by reducing cooking times and helping to serve delicious meals even faster. Try the Cuban-Style Pulled Pork with Olives (page 209), Shrimp & Grits (page 185) and Sesame-Peanut Noodles & Meatballs (page 193).

Slow Cooker

Slow cookers are called "set it and forget it" appliances. Just throw ingredients in the slow cooker in the morning, and it'll cook on low heat (or high heat if you choose) throughout the day and you will have a hot dinner at night. Add Barbecue Brisket Sandwiches with Quick Coleslaw (page 221), Chicken Marbella (page 231) and White Bean Cassoulet with Pork & Lentils (page 239) to your rotation of favorite meals.

Know Your Knives

Chefs swear by this small-but-mighty team. You'll want to be equipped with a chef's knife, a paring knife and a serrated knife.

Chef's Knife The go-to blade for chopping, slicing and dicing. With its pointed tip and hefty rear, it can handle virtually every kitchen chore. There are two styles of chef knives to consider: a Japanese knife and a German knife. Japanese knives are generally lighter. They have thin blades and because of this, they need to be sharpened often to prevent chipping. German knives have thicker blades, making them heavier and bulky, but more sturdy. They require routine sharpening to maintain the blade edge. Look for a knife that feels comfortable in your hand. Chef's knives commonly have 8-inch blades; opt for a 6- or 7-inch one if you have smaller hands.

Paring Knife This little blade is ideal for peeling potatoes, segmenting oranges, slicing mushroom caps and performing other small jobs.

Bread Knife This long serrated blade easily cuts through crusty loaves, flaky desserts and delicate items like soft fruits and vegetables.

Cutting Basics

Many ingredients, such as vegetables, require some prep work! These definitions help you understand what the Test Kitchen chefs suggest in the ingredient lists.

Chop ¼-inch pieces: Coarsely cut up the food, then move the knife through the food until you have the desired size.

Coarsely Chop ½-inch irregular pieces: When chopping, keep the tip of the knife on the cutting board; raise and lower the knife handle in a rocking motion while moving the knife from left to right. If necessary, tuck under the fingers of your opposite hand and carefully push the food toward the blade.

Finely Chop very small (about ⅛ inch) irregular pieces: Start by slicing food, then turn and slice the other way. If you need even smaller pieces, keep the tip of the knife on the cutting board; raise and lower the knife handle in a rocking motion while moving the knife from left to right.

Cube ½-inch blocks: First cut the food lengthwise into ½-inch-thick slices. Stack the slices and cut them into ½-inch-wide sticks, then cut crosswise into ½-inch cubes.

Matchstick thin ⅛-inch by ⅛-inch by 1–2 inch strips: First, cut the food into slices 2 inches long and ⅛-inch thick. Stack the slices and cut them lengthwise into ⅛-inch-wide sticks.

GET A GRIP

Whenever you use your knife, do this: First, grip the blade with your thumb and index finger right above where the blade meets the handle, then wrap the rest of your fingers around the bolster and handle. Now, take your other hand and create a "claw" with fingertips curled under the knuckles pressing down on the food. Your knuckles can then be used as a guide when cutting.

KEEP THEM SHARP

A good, sharp knife is key to cooking well. Not only will it make prep easier, but it's less likely to slip and cut you since a dull knife requires more pressure to use. If you have trouble slicing through ripe tomatoes, it's time to sharpen your knife. To be sure, hold up a piece of paper and attempt to slice through it. A dull knife will dent the edge of the paper while a sharp one will create a long clean cut.

To sharpen a chef knife, you can use a knife sharpener or a whetstone. Many kitchen supply stores also offer knife sharpening services.

Kitchen Tools

::::::::::::::::::::::::::::::

While you may not need all of these items, this list will allow you to tackle most culinary adventures that come your way.

Measuring Cups To measure dry ingredients accurately, use metal or plastic cups that come in nested sets. For liquids, use clear glass or plastic cups with pouring spouts. A 2-cup liquid measuring cup is the most useful.

Measuring Spoons These also come in nesting sets; stainless steel spoons are the most durable. Look for a set that includes a ⅛ teaspoon and a ½ tablespoon though these are hard to find.

Mixing Bowls Glass or ceramic bowls work well and are microwave-safe. Stainless steel bowls are great when you need to quick-chill something, as they react quickly to temperature changes. Plus, they're lightweight.

Tongs Spring-action tongs are the best for picking up foods like salads, vegetables and pasta, and for turning meats without piercing them.

Spatulas & Turners Heatproof silicone spatulas are the favorite for sauce-making. Use heatproof spatulas (pancake turner) to flip food.

Slotted and Wooden Spoons Ideal for mixing ingredients and stirring foods while cooking. A slotted spoon is great for scooping up solid foods and leaving broth or other liquids in the pan, while wooden ones are non-reactive and can safely be used with nonstick cookware.

Vegetable Peelers Swivel-blade peelers come in several configurations and styles, including traditional and Y-handled (a Test Kitchen favorite), with plain, serrated or julienne blades.

Cutting Boards Plastic boards are often lightweight and dishwasher-safe. Hardwood and bamboo boards are extremely durable. They do need to be hand-washed.

Grater This flat, wand, or box-shaped tool can grate, shred or slice. We love a rasp for citrus and hard cheeses.

Citrus Juicer Handheld models make quick work of juicing limes, lemons or oranges.

Food Processor These small appliances chop, shred, blend and mix dough in much less time than it takes to do the same tasks by hand.

Immersion Blender This stick with blender blades on one end is perfect for blending soups or sauces in the pot, taking the messy transfer of foods to a blender out of the equation.

Pepper Grinder Great for adding fast, fresh flavor to meals.

Thermometers These are vital when roasting meats and poultry. Instant-read thermometers, which typically register up to 220°F, are accurate.

Reduce Food Waste

::::::::::::::::::::::::::::

Try these techniques for ensuring that everything you buy will end up on your table—not in the trash.

Plan Each week, think about what you want to cook and flag the most perishable ingredients in each recipe—fresh produce, herbs, dairy products, poultry, seafood. Prioritize selecting a recipe that also uses one (or more!) of those ingredients to cook for lunch or dinner another night that week. Sometimes it makes sense to select just one or two herbs to "spotlight" for the week to avoid an assortment of wilted sprigs.

Experiment Missing an ingredient? Instead of running out to the store, brainstorm a simple substitution and get creative. When cooking, it's best to stick with ingredients similar to what the recipe originally called for, so replace one fresh herb with another, or a splash of oil with a different type of fat.

Freeze, Freeze, Freeze Use small freezer containers such as ice cube trays to make single-serving portions of leftover pasta sauce, pesto, or chopped herbs (covered in olive oil). Toss 'em straight into a hot pan for soups, pastas, sautés and more. Also see Storage Strategies on page 14.

Roast for the Most If you're staring at a refrigerator bin full of sad vegetables, grab a baking sheet and put them in the oven. They'll come out caramelized and tastier than you can imagine and will keep for a couple of additional days in the fridge.

Make a List Have a whiteboard near the fridge on which you keep a running list of everything that is about to go bad. This will encourage you to find creative ways to cook with coconut milk or a jar of pesto rather than let it spoil.

SPRING CHICKEN WITH ASPARAGUS & EDAMAME
131

Storage Strategies

::::::::::::::::::::::::::::::

Follow the "First in, First out" rule. Stock each shelf of your fridge, freezer or pantry as if you worked at a supermarket. When unpacking your shopping bags, always put the newest boxes, cans, and containers behind what's already sitting on the shelf. That way you will reach for the older ones first.

Fill up your fridge. Keep the fridge temperature between 35°F and 38°F. Fruit and vegetables are best kept in the crisper drawers, which can hold in humidity to keep items crisp. Dairy products and eggs should be kept on a shelf—not in the door, where temperatures are too warm. Use the door shelves to store condiments instead.

Clear a shelf. Your freezer probably also holds other food you use on a regular basis (ice cream, frozen fruit for smoothies, etc.). Having one shelf that's dedicated to made-ahead meals will make it easy to store and find things.

Pack up your food. First, let cooked food cool down. Then select your containers. You can use plastic or glass containers (as long as they have airtight lids) or even resealable plastic freezer bags. Quart-size mason jars are great for soups and stews though do not fill them to the top because liquids expand when they freeze and can cause the jar to crack. It's helpful to divide your food into portion sizes that will feed your household so you can defrost only what you need. Individual pieces of food can be wrapped tightly in plastic wrap and then in aluminum foil or placed in a resealable freezer bag.

Label your containers. Here's a restaurant chef tip that's easy to adapt for home use: With a Sharpie, write the name of the dish and the date on a piece of masking tape, then affix the tape to your container before you put it in the freezer.

HOW LONG WILL MEAL-PREPPED FOOD LAST?

Prepared foods can remain refrigerated for 2 to 5 days or frozen for 3 to 4 months, depending on the ingredients. To play it safe and avoid foodborne illness, keep food out of the "danger zone"— temperatures between 40°F and 140°F. Sealing food in airtight packaging or storage containers will not only keep most bacteria out but also protect the flavor and lock moisture in.

Keep Herbs Fresh

Storing herbs properly will make it more likely that you'll use them and cut down on food waste.

Tender Herbs To wash and store delicate herbs like basil and parsley, hold them by the stems and plunge the tops into cold water. Shake to dry, then place the stems in a jar filled with water like a bouquet. Leave basil uncovered and store it at room temperature. To store other tender herbs like parsley and cilantro, loosely cover the well-dried leaves with plastic and place in the fridge.

Woody Herbs To store herbs like rosemary, thyme and oregano, swirl the sprigs around in cold water, then spread them on a clean dish towel to dry.

Wrap the herbs in a slightly damp paper towel. This will keep the leaves protected and hydrated, helping them stay fresh longer.

Store the bundles in an open plastic bag in your fridge's crisper drawer. Check for wilted pieces every few days and replace the paper towels as needed.

Chapter 2

The Dutch Oven

The Dutch oven is the Swiss army knife of pots and pans—it can do it all. From soups and stews to pastas, it's an ideal kitchen workhorse. A quality Dutch oven heats evenly, holds temperature well, is large enough to hold whatever you want to make, cleans easily and lasts a long time—the best models can be passed down from generation to generation.

What is a Dutch oven?

A Dutch oven is a heavy-duty pot designed for searing meat and vegetables and then simmering on the stovetop or braising in the oven. It can also be used for soup and more simple tasks like boiling pasta. It's often used to make no-knead bread as well. Brands like Le Creuset and Staub are some of the best known, while others like Lodge and Cuisinart are standouts as well.

Dutch ovens have wide bases and short, thick walls to allow for browning and caramelization of ingredients and retain heat well. They have two short handles on either side (versus one long on traditional pans) for balanced and steady transferring in and out of the oven. They can also double as serving pieces that keep food warm on the table.

How do I use a Dutch oven?

Dutch ovens can be used the same way you use stockpots or saucepans. The main thing that sets them apart is you can get them really hot to sear meat and then ultimately finish cooking on the stovetop or by transferring to the oven. It's great for gentle braises or long stews on the stovetop.

If I don't have a Dutch oven, what can I use instead?

Instant Pots and other multicookers are essentially electric Dutch ovens. They can be used to brown ingredients and then gently cook them in a contained environment. Slow cookers can also double as Dutch ovens but for some recipes that require searing first, you may need a skillet.

If you don't have either, a good quality saucepan with a lid can work, but chances are it's too small for big batches like these recipes and won't cook as gentle or even. Also double-check the manufacturer's instructions to ensure the pan (and its lid!) are oven-safe.

How to Choose a Dutch Oven

Keep the following features in mind when looking for a Dutch oven and consider which options are the best match for you.

What size Dutch oven do I need?

The standard size for Dutch ovens is about 5½ quarts, but they run anywhere from 8 ounces to 13+ quarts. When buying, consider how many people you cook for as well as the storage space that you have available in your kitchen. Some cooks have their Dutch ovens live on the stove (it will be subjected to a bit more wear and tear here), while others prefer to safely tuck it away in a cabinet between uses.

Smaller sizes (1 to 4 quarts) These sizes are good if you're typically cooking for just yourself and/or one other person. They are easy to maneuver, clean and transport, but they may not be suitable for larger dishes or entertaining. Even smaller sizes, like 8 ounces, are good for individual servings and presentation.

Medium sizes (5 to 7 quarts) Five and a half quarts is a popular size and good for the first-time buyer. It can handle family-sized batches yet isn't too heavy and cumbersome to handle.

Larger sizes (8 to 13 quarts) These sizes are great for large families, special occasions and big-batch cooking. Keep in mind, the bigger your Dutch oven is, the heavier and more difficult to maneuver it will be.

What are Dutch ovens made of?

Dutch ovens are often made out of heavy cast iron, which has the ability to get very hot and maintain temperature well. They can also be made out of other materials like stainless steel and ceramic.

Is an enamel coating necessary?

An enamel coating allows for easier cleaning and maintenance and delivers all of the browning benefits of cast iron without having to season it. (Fun fact: Enameled Dutch ovens are actually French ovens, but this type has become so popular that it's become synonymous with the Dutch oven we know and love.) Skip other nonstick materials when it comes to Dutch ovens: they don't typically allow for cooking on high heat and developing the brown bits that are found on the bottom of the pot, which contribute to flavor.

What shape is best for me?

Most Dutch ovens are round; however, they're also available in oval shapes and some festive holiday and seasonal shapes. When it comes to shape, here's what to keep in mind:

A round shape These fit more symmetrically on top of a burner. If you are going to be doing a lot of stovetop cooking, then it is advantageous to stick to a round shape so that you don't have to worry about any parts of the pot heating unevenly over the burner.

Oval shapes Oval Dutch ovens can better accommodate a whole chicken or a large cut of meat because of the added length that they offer. Sometimes the ends of an oval Dutch oven might not get as hot as the center. That said, if you have an induction stove, you can position an oval Dutch oven over two synced burners for more even heating.

Other shapes, like pumpkins and tomatoes While these novelty shapes are great for entertaining, from a practical everyday standpoint, they don't offer much more than an appealing aesthetic due to their curves and lid handle.

What other features should I look for?

Look for the following additional features for ease of usability.

A tight-fitting lid While this might not seem like a make-or-break characteristic for a Dutch oven, the shape and size of the lid is definitely something to consider. The lid should fit the pot securely, yet still allow some steam to escape so that moisture can cook off in soups and stews. A glass lid is useful if you like to keep an eye on your food without losing heat.

Roomy handles The shape of the handle should be something that's easy for you to grab with an oven mitt or kitchen towel (keep in mind that the shorter the handle, the quicker it will get hot). Large handles are nice for stabilizing the pot while you're stirring, and they make the pot much easier to maneuver when you're cleaning it.

HEARTY BEAN &
BEEF CHILI
23

GH
KITCHEN
APPLIANCES
LAB

TOP-TESTED DUTCH OVENS

The Kitchen Appliances Lab tests Dutch ovens to understand how each heats, cooks and cleans. We did this by cooking 48 pounds of beef stew meat, 7½ pounds of onions, 6 pounds of carrots, 12 quarts of chicken broth and 11 bottles of red wine. The procedures include performance evaluations to determine the evenness of heat distribution on gas and electric ranges, the ability to simmer steadily, the tenderness of meat and the quality of the resulting beef stew. At cleanup, we note whether the pots stain or chip when clunked against the side of the sink (it happens).

BEST OVERALL
Le Creuset Round Dutch Oven
In addition to a sleek design and a wide array of color options, this Dutch oven delivers when it comes to performance and durability. In our tests, it cooked a good beef stew with even browning throughout and the handles stayed cool enough to grasp without a potholder. At 11½ pounds, it's relatively lightweight, and the large knob on the lid stays cool and makes it easy to handle. Its lifetime warranty makes it an investment piece that's worth it.

**SCAN FOR MORE
DUTCH OVEN
LAB REVIEWS**

Cooking Tips for Best Results

::::::::::::::::::::::::::

1. **Cut food into evenly sized pieces.** This will ensure they cook evenly and no one chances a bite that's underdone.

2. **For a deep sear, heat the pot first.** Then add a little bit of oil just before adding in the meat. This will help prevent the oil from overheating and burning.

3. **Sear meat and then vegetables.** First cook the meat and then remove it to a plate. Then turn down the heat and add the vegetables. This will impart the flavor of the meat to the vegetables and allow them to cook at their own, more gentle pace.

4. **Brown large amounts of meat in batches.** This will help prevent steam buildup, which makes meat tough. Drain any excess grease in between batches.

5. **Use kosher salt.** Salting meat and vegetables before cooking helps release moisture and allows for better color and flavor.

6. **Always season to taste.** When food simmers or braises, its flavors become very concentrated.

7. **Deglaze after browning.** This will loosen the brown bits that have formed on the bottom of the pot and deepen the flavor of a pan sauce or stew.

8. **Keep the pot covered.** While making soups and other foods, you want to cook gently, covering the pan to keep the moisture contained within the pot. Careful, the lid's handle may get hot, especially if it's made of metal.

9. **Leave the lid ajar when making sauce.** This allows for some evaporation and concentration of flavor. And don't use it when trying to reduce liquid in the final stages of cooking.

HOW TO FREEZE AND REHEAT SOUPS AND STEWS

Cool in containers, uncovered, on the counter until room temperature. Cover containers tightly; label and freeze up to 3 months.

When ready to serve, place frozen soup, still in the covered container, up to its rim in a bowl or sink of hot water for 1 to 3 minutes or until the sides separate from the container. Invert into a saucepan or skillet and add ¼ to ½ cup water. Cover and bring to a boil, stirring occasionally; boil 1 minute, stirring.

Or, invert into microwave-safe bowl or baking dish; cover with parchment paper or vented plastic wrap. Heat in microwave on Defrost until most of the ice crystals are gone and the soup can be easily stirred. Then heat on high until it reaches 165°F on an instant-read thermometer, stirring gently once during heating.

◄ French Onion Soup

3 tablespoons olive oil

4 pounds yellow onions (about 5 large onions), thinly sliced

Kosher salt

1½ teaspoons all-purpose flour

¼ cup cognac or dry white wine

8 cups low-sodium beef broth

2 bay leaves

6 large thyme sprigs, plus thyme leaves for topping

1 tablespoon sherry vinegar

8 thin slices country bread

3 ounces Gruyère cheese, finely shredded

ACTIVE TIME 50 min. | **TOTAL TIME** 1 hr. 50 min. | **SERVES** 4

1. Heat the oil in a large Dutch oven on medium. Add the onions and 1½ teaspoons salt, reduce the heat to low, and cook, stirring occasionally, until the onions are tender and have released their liquid, 10 minutes.

2. Increase the heat to medium-high and continue cooking, stirring often and scraping the bottom of the pot, until the onions are deep brown and caramelized, 40 to 50 minutes. If the bottom of the pot starts to get too dark, add 4 to 5 tablespoons water.

3. Sprinkle the onions with the flour and cook, stirring, 2 minutes. Stir in the cognac and cook for 1 minute. Add the broth, bay leaves and thyme, and simmer until reduced to about 8 cups, 18 to 20 minutes. Discard the herbs and stir in the vinegar.

4. When ready to serve, heat the broiler. Arrange the bread on a rimmed baking sheet and sprinkle with the Gruyère and some fresh thyme leaves. Broil in the top third of the oven until golden brown and bubbling, about 1 minute. Serve the cheese toasts on top of the soup.

PER SERVING *About 440 calories, 20 g fat (5.5 g saturated fat), 15 g protein, 1,255 mg sodium, 53 g carbohydrates, 8 g fiber*

⇒ FAMILY FRIENDLY ⇐

Hearty Bean & Beef Chili

2 tablespoons olive oil, divided

1 pound ground beef

2 teaspoons ground cumin

2 teaspoons chili powder

Kosher salt and pepper

1 yellow onion, finely chopped

1 garlic clove, pressed

1 pound tomatoes, finely chopped

1 15-ounce can cannellini beans, rinsed

ACTIVE TIME 30 min. | **TOTAL TIME** 40 min. | **SERVES** 4

1. Heat 1 tablespoon of the oil in a large Dutch oven on medium. Add the beef, cumin, chili powder and ½ teaspoon each salt and pepper and cook, breaking up the beef, until browned, about 10 minutes. Transfer the beef to a paper towel–lined plate.

2. Return the pot to medium; add the remaining tablespoon olive oil, then the onion, and cook until tender, 4 to 5 minutes. Stir in the garlic and cook for 1 minute. Add the tomatoes and cook until they release their juices, about 5 minutes. Add 2 cups water and simmer until slightly thickened, about 10 minutes.

3. Transfer half of the beans to a small bowl and mash with a fork. Add to the pot along with the whole beans and the reserved beef and heat through.

PER SERVING *About 375 calories, 17 g fat (4.5 g saturated fat), 30 g protein, 480 mg sodium, 25 g carbohydrates, 11 g fiber*

2 tablespoons olive oil

1 large onion, chopped

1 large red pepper, chopped

½ teaspoon salt

2 cloves garlic, papery skin removed

1 jalapeño, stem and seeds removed

1 1-inch piece ginger, peeled

2 teaspoons ground coriander

1 teaspoon ground cumin

2½ pounds tomatoes,
  roughly chopped

2½ cups water

2 pocketless pitas

1 tablespoon brown sugar

2 tablespoons butter or olive oil

2 tablespoons finely shredded
  unsweetened coconut

2 tablespoons cilantro, chopped

Spiced Fresh Tomato Soup with Sweet & Herby Pitas

ACTIVE TIME 15 min. | **TOTAL TIME** 25 min. | **SERVES** 4

1. Heat olive oil in large Dutch oven on medium-low. Add onion, red pepper and salt, and cook, covered, stirring occasionally, until tender, 8 to 10 minutes.

2. Meanwhile, finely grate the garlic, jalapeño and ginger. Add to the onion mixture and cook, stirring, for 1 minute. Stir in the ground coriander and ground cumin and cook for 1 minute.

3. Add the tomatoes and water; increase the heat to medium and simmer, partially covered, for 10 minutes. While the tomatoes are cooking, toast 2 pocketless pitas.

4. Using an immersion blender (or standard blender, in batches), puree the soup until smooth.

5. Combine the brown sugar in bowl with the butter, coconut and cilantro. Spread onto the toasted pitas, then cut and serve with the soup.

PER SERVING *About 324 calories, 16 g fat (7 g saturated fat), 6 g protein, 563 mg sodium, 43 g carbohydrates, 7 g fiber*

4 large leeks

2 to 4 garlic cloves, unpeeled

Kosher salt and ground black pepper

1 large all-purpose potato, peeled, cut
   lengthwise in half, and thinly sliced

1 small fennel bulb, trimmed and
   chopped (optional)

3 parsnips, peeled and thinly sliced

2 large carrots, thinly sliced

3 stalks celery with leaves,
   thinly sliced

4 ounces mushrooms, trimmed
   and thinly sliced

10 parsley sprigs

4 thyme sprigs

2 bay leaves

1 teaspoon whole black peppercorns

Vegetable Broth

ACTIVE TIME 25 min. | **TOTAL TIME** 2 hr. | **MAKES** 5½ cups

1. Cut off the roots and trim the dark green tops from the leeks; thinly slice the leeks. Rinse the leeks in a large bowl of cold water, swishing to remove any sand. Transfer to a colander to drain, leaving the sand in the bottom of the bowl.

2. In a 6-quart saucepot, combine the leeks, garlic, 1 cup water and a pinch of salt; bring to a boil. Reduce the heat to medium, cover and cook until the leeks are tender, about 15 minutes.

3. Add the potato, fennel if using, parsnips, carrots, celery, mushrooms, parsley, thyme, bay leaves, peppercorns and 12 cups water. Bring to a boil; reduce the heat and simmer, uncovered, for at least 1 hour 30 minutes.

4. Taste and continue cooking if the flavor is not concentrated enough. Season with salt and ground pepper to taste. Strain the broth through a fine-mesh sieve into containers, pressing on the solids with back of wooden spoon to extract liquid; cool. Cover and refrigerate to use within 3 days, or freeze for up to 4 months.

PER CUP *About 19 calories, 0 g fat (0 g saturated fat), 1 g protein,*
9 mg sodium, 4 g carbohydrates, 0 g fiber

1 3- to 3½-pound chicken,
   including neck (reserve giblets
   for another use)

2 carrots, cut into 2-inch pieces

1 stalk celery, cut into 2-inch pieces

1 medium onion, unpeeled and cut
   into quarters

5 parsley sprigs

1 garlic clove, unpeeled

1 teaspoon dried thyme

1 bay leaf

Chicken Broth

ACTIVE TIME 10 min. | **TOTAL TIME** 4 hr. 30 min. | **MAKES** About 5½ cups

1. In a 6-quart saucepot, combine the chicken, chicken neck, carrots, celery, onion, parsley, garlic, thyme, bay leaf and 3 quarts water or enough water to cover; bring to a boil on high. With a slotted spoon, skim any foam from the surface. Reduce the heat to low, cover, and simmer, turning the chicken once and skimming foam occasionally, for 1 hour.

2. Remove from the heat; transfer the chicken to a large bowl. When cool enough to handle, remove the skin and bones from the chicken. (Reserve the meat for another use.) Return the skin and bones to the pot and bring to a boil on high. Skim any foam. Reduce the heat to low and simmer, uncovered, for 3 hours.

3. Strain the broth through a colander into a large bowl; discard solids. Strain again through a sieve into containers; cool. Cover and refrigerate to use within 3 days, or freeze for up to 4 months.

4. To use, skim and discard fat from the surface of the broth.

PER CUP *About 36 calories, 1 g fat (1 g saturated fat), 3 g protein,*
91 mg sodium, 4 g carbohydrates, 0 g fiber

1 pound ground pork

1 teaspoon ground cumin

1 teaspoon ground coriander

½ teaspoon ancho chili powder

Kosher salt and pepper

1 tablespoon olive oil

1 onion, thinly sliced

½ bunch cilantro, stems and
    leaves separated

4 cups low-sodium chicken broth

1 14-ounce can diced tomatoes

1 29-ounce can hominy, rinsed

2 tablespoons lime juice, plus lime
    wedges for serving

Sliced radishes, for serving

‹ Pork & Hominy Soup

ACTIVE TIME 20 min. | **TOTAL TIME** 30 min. | **SERVES** 4

1. In a bowl, toss the pork with the cumin, coriander, chili powder, ¼ teaspoon salt and ½ teaspoon pepper.

2. Heat the oil in a large Dutch oven on medium. Add the pork and onion and cook, breaking up the pork into small pieces, until browned, 6 to 8 minutes.

3. Meanwhile, finely chop the cilantro stems. Add to the pot and cook, stirring, for 1 minute. Add the chicken broth and tomatoes (and their juices), cover, and bring to a boil. Add the hominy, reduce heat, and simmer for 10 minutes.

4. Stir in the lime juice. Serve with cilantro leaves, radishes, and lime wedges if desired.

PER SERVING *About 475 calories, 23 g fat (6.5 g saturated fat), 30 g protein, 1,044 mg sodium, 45 g carbohydrates, 7 g fiber*

---

1 pound hot Italian sausage links,
    casings pierced with a fork

3 tablespoons vegetable oil

2 cups all-purpose flour

2 medium stalks celery, cut into
    2-inch pieces

1 medium green bell pepper, cut into
    2-inch pieces

1 medium onion, cut into 2-inch pieces

1¾ cups chicken broth

1 10-ounce package frozen whole
    okra, thawed

2 teaspoons hot pepper sauce

2 teaspoons dried thyme

2 teaspoons dried oregano

1 bay leaf

1 pound large shrimp, shelled and
    deveined, with tails left on

Cooked long-grain white rice,
    for serving

Oregano sprigs, for topping (optional)

Shrimp & Sausage Gumbo

ACTIVE TIME 10 min. | **TOTAL TIME** 40 min. | **SERVES** 6

1. Heat a large Dutch oven on medium-high until hot. Add the sausages and cook, turning often, until very brown, about 10 minutes. With a slotted spoon, transfer the sausages to a plate to cool slightly. Cut each sausage crosswise into thirds.

2. Discard all but 1 tablespoon of the drippings from the Dutch oven. Add the oil and heat on medium until hot. Stir in the flour until blended and cook, stirring frequently, until the flour is dark brown but not burned. Add the celery, green pepper, and onion and cook, stirring occasionally, until tender, 8 to 10 minutes.

3. Return the sausages to the Dutch oven. Gradually stir in the chicken broth, okra, hot pepper sauce, thyme, dried oregano, bay leaf and ½ cup water; bring to a boil. Reduce the heat to low, cover, and simmer for 15 minutes. Add the shrimp and cook, uncovered, until the shrimp turn opaque throughout, about 2 minutes. Remove and discard the bay leaf.

4. To serve, divide the rice equally among 6 bowls and top with gumbo. Top with oregano sprigs, if you like.

PER SERVING *About 495 calories, 25 g fat (7 g saturated fat), 29 g protein, 820 mg sodium, 38 g carbohydrates, 2 g fiber*

TIP Keep this a one-pot recipe and prepare frozen rice in the microwave.

1 medium onion, quartered

1 leek, white and light green parts only, cut into 1-inch pieces

1 stalk celery, cut into 1-inch pieces

3 tablespoons low-sodium chicken bouillon base (we like Better Than Bouillon)

1 bone-in chicken breast (about 2½ pounds), split

1 small oregano sprig

¼ small bunch dill, plus sprigs for serving

½ cup long-grain white rice

2 large eggs

6 tablespoons lemon juice

Cracked pepper, for serving

Greek Lemon Chicken Soup

ACTIVE TIME 25 min. | **TOTAL TIME** 45 min. | **SERVES** 4

1. In a large Dutch oven, combine the onion, leek, celery and bouillon with 10 cups water and bring to a boil. Reduce the heat, add the chicken, oregano and dill and simmer until the chicken is just cooked through, 15 to 20 minutes.

2. Transfer the chicken to a bowl and, when cool enough to handle, shred the meat, discarding the skin and bones.

3. Strain the liquid and return it to the pot. Add the rice and simmer for 12 minutes.

4. Meanwhile, in a medium bowl, whisk together the eggs and lemon juice until foamy and combined.

5. Ladle 1 cup of hot broth off the top of the soup into a measuring cup. Slowly whisk this broth, 1 tablespoon at a time, into the egg mixture. Then, whisking constantly, gradually add this egg-broth mixture to the pot. Simmer until the soup is slightly thickened and velvety and the rice is tender, about 5 minutes. Remove from the heat and stir in the shredded chicken. Serve topped with dill and pepper.

PER SERVING *About 440 calories, 13 g fat (3.5 g saturated fat), 52 g protein, 1,260 mg sodium, 26 g carbohydrates, 0 g fiber*

TIP Whisked eggs and lemon juice, tempered with a little hot broth to prevent scrambling, add ultra-velvety texture to the soup without using any cream.

4 large ears corn, shucked

2½ pounds bone-in chicken breasts, skin removed

Kosher salt and pepper

4 tablespoons butter

1 tablespoon olive oil

5 stalks celery, chopped

4 large carrots, chopped

1 medium onion, finely chopped

⅓ cup all-purpose flour

½ cup half-and-half

3 tablespoons chopped fresh tarragon

◄ Creamy Chicken-Corn Chowder

ACTIVE TIME 15 min. | **TOTAL TIME** 1 hr. 5 min. | **SERVES** 8

1. Cut the corn kernels from the cobs; set kernels aside. Scrape the juices from the cobs into a Dutch oven; add the cobs, along with 8 cups water, the chicken, and ½ teaspoon salt. Bring to a boil on high. Reduce the heat to maintain a gentle simmer. Cook for 20 to 25 minutes or until the chicken is cooked, turning the chicken occasionally. Remove the pot from heat and let it cool. Transfer the chicken to a large bowl. When it is cool enough to handle, remove and discard any bones; pull the meat into bite-size pieces. Remove and discard the cobs from the poaching liquid; reserve the liquid.

2. In the Dutch oven, heat the butter and oil on medium until the butter has melted. Add the celery, carrots, onion and ½ teaspoon salt. Cook for 10 minutes or until the vegetables are beginning to soften, stirring frequently.

3. Sprinkle the flour over the vegetables; cook for 1 minute, stirring. Stir in the reserved poaching liquid and the corn kernels. Bring to a boil on high; boil for 1 minute, stirring. Reduce the heat to maintain a simmer. Cook for 15 minutes, stirring occasionally. Stir in the half-and-half, tarragon, reserved chicken, 1 teaspoon salt and ½ teaspoon pepper.

PER SERVING *About 300 calories, 13 g fat (6 g saturated fat), 25 g protein, 645 mg sodium, 24 g carbohydrates, 3 g fiber*

2 tablespoons olive oil

2 stalks celery, thinly sliced

1 large onion, finely chopped

1 large carrot, cut into ¼-inch pieces

2 garlic cloves, finely chopped

½ teaspoon red pepper flakes

1 pound russet potatoes, cut into ½-inch pieces

3 thyme sprigs

1 28-ounce can whole tomatoes

2 8-ounce bottles clam juice

½ cup dry white wine

2 6½-ounce cans chopped clams, drained

¼ cup chopped fresh flat-leaf parsley

Crusty bread, for serving (optional)

≋ QUICK & EASY ≋

Manhattan Clam Chowder

ACTIVE TIME 25 min. | **TOTAL TIME** 30 min. | **SERVES** 6

1. Heat the oil in a large pot or Dutch oven on medium. Add the celery, onion and carrot and cook, covered, stirring occasionally, until tender, 8 to 10 minutes. Stir in the garlic and red pepper flakes and cook 1 minute.

2. Add the potatoes, thyme, tomatoes and their juice (crushing tomatoes as you add), clam juice, white wine and ½ cup water and bring to a boil. Reduce the heat and simmer until the potatoes are tender, 8 to 10 minutes. Stir in clams to heat through.

3. Sprinkle with the parsley and serve with bread if desired.

PER SERVING *About 305 calories, 8 g fat (1 g saturated fat), 20 g protein, 800 mg sodium, 37 g carbohydrates, 6 g fiber*

Creamy Chickpea Soup

1 tablespoon olive oil

1 large onion, thinly sliced

2 large carrots, chopped

1 leek, white and light green parts only, sliced

1 garlic clove, sliced

Kosher salt

2 15-ounce cans low-sodium chickpeas, rinsed

4 cups low-sodium vegetable broth

ACTIVE TIME 30 min. | **TOTAL TIME** 40 min. | **SERVES** 4

1. Heat the olive oil in a large Dutch oven on medium. Add the onion, carrots, leek, garlic and ½ teaspoon salt and cook, covered, stirring occasionally, for 5 minutes.

2. Add all but ¼ cup of the chickpeas and cook, covered, stirring occasionally, until the vegetables are tender, 5 to 6 minutes.

3. Add the vegetable broth and 2 cups water and bring to a boil, then reduce the heat and simmer until the vegetables are very tender, 10 to 12 minutes. Remove from the heat.

4. While the soup simmers, roughly chop the remaining ¼ cup chickpeas.

5. With an immersion blender or a standard blender, in batches, puree the soup until very smooth. Top with the reserved chickpeas and the optional paprika oil.

PER SERVING About 310 calories, 10.5 g fat (1.5 g saturated fat), 11 g protein, 555 mg sodium, 45 g carbohydrates, 12 g fiber

Coq au Vin Rosé

4 ounces pancetta, cut into ½-inch pieces

2 teaspoons olive oil

1 3½- to 4-pound chicken, cut into 10 pieces

Kosher salt and pepper

1 pound cremini mushrooms, quartered

2 medium onions, finely chopped

2 leeks (white and light green parts only), halved and sliced

2 garlic cloves, pressed

2 tablespoons all-purpose flour

1 750-ml bottle dry rosé wine

½ cup low-sodium chicken broth

2 tablespoons Dijon mustard

6 thyme sprigs

2 bay leaves

¼ cup chopped fresh tarragon

ACTIVE TIME 45 min. | **TOTAL TIME** 2 hr. 15 min. | **SERVES** 6

1. Heat the oven to 350°F. Heat a large Dutch oven on medium. Add the pancetta and oil and cook until the pancetta is browned, 3 minutes. Using a slotted spoon, transfer it to a paper towel.

2. Pat the chicken pieces very dry and season with ½ teaspoon each salt and pepper. Add the chicken, skin side down, to the pot and cook until golden brown, 5 minutes per side. Transfer to a plate.

3. Increase the heat to medium-high, then add the mushrooms and cook, tossing only twice, until browned, 6 to 8 minutes. Reduce the heat to medium-low and add the onions, leeks and garlic and cook, stirring occasionally, until light golden brown and tender, 6 to 7 minutes.

4. Sprinkle the vegetables with the flour and cook, stirring, 1 minute. Add the wine and bring to a simmer. Stir in the broth, mustard, thyme and bay leaves.

5. Return the chicken and pancetta to the Dutch oven, cover, transfer to the oven, and cook until the chicken is fork-tender, about 1½ hours. Remove from the oven, discard the thyme and bay leaves and sprinkle with tarragon.

PER SERVING About 535 calories, 33.5 g fat (9.5 g saturated fat), 40 g protein, 585 mg sodium, 18 g carbohydrates, 2 g fiber

1 medium onion, chopped

2 tablespoons chili powder

1 tablespoon canola oil

Kosher salt

1 28-ounce can crushed tomatoes

1 15-ounce can black beans, rinsed

1 pound macaroni, cooked

1 cup shredded sharp Cheddar cheese

Chopped fresh cilantro, for topping

≒ VEGETARIAN ≒

‹ Chili Macaroni

ACTIVE TIME 15 min. | **TOTAL TIME** 20 min. | **SERVES** 6

1. In a large Dutch oven, cook the onion, chili powder, canola oil and ½ teaspoon salt on medium for 8 minutes, stirring often. Add the crushed tomatoes and black beans.

2. Bring to a simmer on high; simmer for 5 minutes. Toss with the cooked macaroni and the Cheddar. Top with the cilantro.

PER SERVING *About 500 calories, 11 g fat (4 g saturated fat), 22 g protein, 770 mg sodium, 82 g carbohydrates, 11 g fiber*

MAKE IT VEGAN Omit sharp Cheddar or replace with dairy-alternative cheese.

1 tablespoon olive oil

6 garlic cloves, pressed

1 tablespoon grated lemon zest

½ teaspoon fennel seeds, crushed

¼ teaspoon red pepper flakes

1 tablespoon tomato paste

Kosher salt

1 bunch kale, stems and tough ribs removed, leaves coarsely chopped (about 12 cups)

2 pints grape or cherry tomatoes

1 15-ounce can low-sodium chickpeas, rinsed

Lemon wedges and grated Pecorino cheese, for serving (optional)

≒ QUICK & EASY ≒

Quick Chickpea & Kale Stew

ACTIVE TIME 25 min. | **TOTAL TIME** 25 min. | **SERVES** 4

1. Heat the oil in a large Dutch oven on medium. Add the garlic and lemon zest and cook, stirring, for 1 minute.

2. Add fennel seeds and red pepper flakes and cook, stirring, 2 minutes more. Stir in tomato paste and cook for 1 minute.

3. Add 4 cups water and 1 teaspoon salt; cover and bring to a boil. Add the kale, tomatoes and chickpeas and simmer for 4 minutes.

4. Uncover and cook, stirring, until the kale is just tender and the tomatoes have begun to break down, 2 to 3 minutes more. Serve with lemon wedges and Pecorino if desired.

PER SERVING *About 185 calories, 6 g fat (0.5 g saturated fat), 9 g protein, 580 mg sodium, 28 g carbohydrates, 8 g fiber*

2 tablespoons olive oil

1 large onion, chopped

6 garlic cloves, pressed

1 red chile, finely chopped

2 tablespoons finely grated
   peeled fresh ginger

1 tablespoon garam masala

1 tablespoon ground coriander

2 teaspoons sweet paprika

Kosher salt and pepper

2 tablespoons tomato paste

1½ pounds boneless, skinless chicken
   breasts, cut into 2-inch chunks

1 cup Chicken Broth
   (see page 25)

¼ cup plain full-fat yogurt, plus
   more for serving

Cooked rice, for serving

Chopped fresh cilantro,
   for topping (optional)

‹ Traditional Chicken Curry

ACTIVE TIME 30 min. | **TOTAL TIME** 30 min. | **SERVES** 6

1. Heat the oil in a large Dutch oven on medium-high. Add the onion and cook, stirring occasionally, until it begins to change color. Reduce the heat to medium and cook, stirring occasionally, until the onion is tender, 3 to 4 minutes more.

2. Stir in the garlic and chile and cook for 1 minute. Stir in the ginger, garam masala, coriander, paprika and ½ teaspoon salt and cook, stirring, for 2 minutes.

3. Stir in the tomato paste and cook for 2 minutes. Season the chicken with ½ teaspoon each salt and pepper, then add to the pot and cook, tossing occasionally, until it is no longer pink, 5 minutes. Stir in the chicken broth and gently simmer, covered, until the chicken is cooked through, 6 to 8 minutes.

4. Stir in the yogurt and serve over rice, sprinkled with cilantro if desired.

PER SERVING *About 220 calories, 8.5 fat (1.5 g saturated fat), 28 g protein, 395 mg sodium, 8 g carbohydrates, 2 g fiber*

1 tablespoon olive oil

1 large onion, chopped

3 garlic cloves, finely chopped

2 teaspoons chili powder

1 cup salsa

1 cup Chicken Broth
   (see page 25)

½ cup Nutella

2 pounds bone-in chicken thighs
   and legs, skin removed

Kosher salt

Cooked yellow rice, for serving

Sesame seeds and sliced scallions,
   for topping (optional)

Chicken Mole

ACTIVE TIME 15 min. | **TOTAL TIME** 45 min. | **SERVES** 4

1. Heat the oil in a large Dutch oven on medium. Add the onion, garlic and chili powder and cook until softened, stirring often, about 7 minutes.

2. Stir in the salsa and chicken broth, then whisk in the Nutella.

3. Season the chicken with ½ teaspoon salt and add it to the pot. Simmer until the chicken is tender and cooked through, about 30 minutes. Serve with yellow rice, sprinkled with sesame seeds and scallions if desired.

PER SERVING *About 355 calories, 17.5 g fat (4.5 g saturated fat), 25 g protein, 1,015 mg sodium, 26 g carbohydrates, 4 g fiber*

TIP Got leftovers? Shred the chicken and tuck it into tacos, burritos or cheesy quesadillas.

1 tablespoon olive oil

2 ounces Spanish (cured) chorizo, thinly sliced

2 stalks celery, thinly sliced

1 fennel bulb, cored and thinly sliced

2 garlic cloves, thinly sliced

1 28-ounce can whole peeled tomatoes in juice

¾ cup dry white wine

1 12-ounce cod fillet, cut into 2-inch pieces

½ pound large peeled and deveined shrimp

1 tablespoon red wine vinegar

1 tablespoon chopped fresh tarragon

Crusty bread, for serving (optional)

Seafood, Chorizo & Vegetable Stew

ACTIVE TIME 20 min. | **TOTAL TIME** 20 min. | **SERVES** 4

1. Heat the oil in a large Dutch oven on medium-high. Add the chorizo and cook, stirring, for 1 minute.

2. Add the celery, fennel and garlic and cook, covered, stirring occasionally, until the vegetables are beginning to soften, 3 to 4 minutes.

3. Crush the tomatoes and add them to the pan along with their juices. Add the wine and bring to a boil. Add the cod and shrimp and cook, covered, stirring once, until the seafood is opaque throughout, 3 to 4 minutes. Remove from the heat and stir in the vinegar and tarragon. Serve with bread if desired.

PER SERVING *About 280 calories, 10 g fat (3 g saturated fat), 29 g protein, 1,025 mg sodium, 16 g carbohydrates, 4 g fiber*

---

3 tablespoons coconut or canola oil, divided

½ small butternut squash (about 1 pound), peeled and cut into ½-inch pieces (about 2½ cups)

1 onion, chopped

2 garlic cloves, finely chopped

1 tablespoon grated peeled fresh ginger

3 tablespoons yellow Thai curry paste

1 14-ounce can light coconut milk

1 jalapeño, halved

½ teaspoon ground turmeric

1 red bell pepper, seeded and cut into ½-inch pieces

2 tablespoons lime juice, plus lime wedges for serving

1 tablespoon fish sauce

3 cups baby spinach, chopped

Cooked long-grain white rice, for serving

Chopped cashews and fresh cilantro, for topping (optional)

Butternut Squash Coconut Curry

ACTIVE TIME 35 min. | **TOTAL TIME** 45 min. | **SERVES** 4

1. Heat 2 tablespoons of the oil in a large Dutch oven on medium. Add the squash and cook, tossing occasionally, until golden brown and beginning to soften, 4 to 6 minutes; transfer the squash to a plate.

2. Add the remaining 1 tablespoon oil along with the onion and sauté for 6 minutes. Stir in the garlic and ginger and cook for 2 minutes. Add the curry paste and cook, stirring, for 1 minute.

3. Add the coconut milk, jalapeño and turmeric and bring to a simmer. Add the bell pepper and squash and simmer until the squash is just tender, about 15 minutes. Remove from the heat, remove and discard the jalapeño and stir in the lime juice and fish sauce. Then fold in the spinach to wilt. Serve over the rice and sprinkle with cashews and cilantro if desired.

PER SERVING *About 460 calories, 18.5 g fat (15 g saturated fat), 9 g protein, 855 mg sodium, 64 g carbohydrates, 5 g fiber*

1 lemon

12 ounces spaghetti

1 small red onion, thinly sliced

½ cup dry white wine

2 tablespoons olive oil

2 garlic cloves, thinly sliced

Kosher salt and pepper

1½ pints assorted color cherry or
grape tomatoes, halved

½ cup roughly chopped fresh
flat-leaf parsley

1 cup roughly chopped fresh basil

Grated Parmesan cheese or vegan
Parmesan alternative, for
topping (optional)

⇒ QUICK & EASY ⇐

‹ One-Pot Spaghetti

ACTIVE TIME 20 min. | **TOTAL TIME** 20 min. | **SERVES** 4

1. Peel 4 strips of zest from the lemon and thinly slice, then squeeze 2 tablespoons juice.

2. In a large skillet or Dutch oven, place the spaghetti (it should lie flat on the bottom). Add 4 cups water, the lemon juice, onion, wine, oil, garlic, ¾ teaspoon salt and ½ teaspoon pepper. Bring to a boil and boil gently, stirring frequently, 5 minutes.

3. Fold in the tomatoes and continue to boil gently until the pasta is al dente and nearly all the liquid has been absorbed (absorption will continue).

4. Stir in the lemon zest and parsley, then fold in the basil. Serve with Parmesan if desired.

PER SERVING *About 430 calories, 9 g fat (1.5 g saturated fat), 14 g protein, 385 mg sodium, 73 g carbohydrates, 6 g fiber*

2 tablespoons olive oil, plus
more for serving

1 large onion

Kosher salt and pepper

2 garlic cloves, pressed

2 tablespoons tomato paste

4 carrots, chopped

2 stalks celery, chopped

1 russet potato, chopped

6 thyme sprigs (optional)

½ head savoy cabbage, chopped

1 cup ditalini pasta, cooked

1 15-ounce can white beans, rinsed

2 cups baby spinach

Grated Parmesan cheese, for topping

Crusty bread, for serving (optional)

⇒ VEGETARIAN ⇐

Classic Minestrone

ACTIVE TIME 25 min. | **TOTAL TIME** 45 min. | **SERVES** 6

1. Heat the oil in a large Dutch oven on medium. Add the onion, season with ¼ teaspoon each salt and pepper, and cook, covered, stirring occasionally, until the onion is very tender, 8 to 10 minutes. Stir in the garlic and cook for 1 minute. Add the tomato paste and cook, stirring, 2 minutes.

2. Add the carrots, celery, potato, thyme (if using) and 8 cups water and bring to a boil. Reduce the heat and simmer for 10 minutes. Add the cabbage and simmer until the vegetables are tender, 10 to 12 minutes more.

3. Discard the thyme. Stir the pasta and beans into the soup and cook until the beans are heated through, about 3 minutes. Remove from the heat and add the spinach, folding until it is beginning to wilt. Serve with additional olive oil, Parmesan and crusty bread if desired.

PER SERVING *About 264 calories, 5 g fat (1 g saturated fat), 10 g protein, 567 mg sodium, 46 g carbohydrates, 8 g fiber*

TIP Add leftover Parmesan rinds to the soup. They lend a subtle cheesy flavor as the soup simmers.

MAKE IT VEGAN Omit Parmesan cheese.

2 tablespoons olive oil

4 garlic cloves, finely chopped

¼ teaspoon red pepper flakes

2 cups dry white wine

Kosher salt

4 pounds mussels, scrubbed and
    beards removed

3 tablespoons unsalted butter, cold

¼ cup roughly chopped fresh
    flat-leaf parsley

Crusty bread and lemon wedges,
    for serving (optional)

White Wine Mussels

ACTIVE TIME 20 min. | **TOTAL TIME** 20 min. | **SERVES** 4

1. Heat the oil with the garlic and red pepper flakes in a large Dutch oven on medium-low until the garlic is beginning to turn golden brown, 4 minutes. Add the wine and bring to a boil on medium-high, then boil 2 minutes.

2. Add ¼ teaspoon salt, then the mussels, and cook, covered, stirring once or twice, until the shells open, 6 minutes. Uncover, add the butter, and cook for 2 minutes, stirring. Toss with parsley and serve with crusty bread and lemon wedges if desired.

PER SERVING *About 280 calories, 18.5 g fat (7 g saturated fat), 17 g protein, 515 mg sodium, 10 g carbohydrates, 0 g fiber*

Mix it up!

For flavor variations below, follow the above directions, sautéing seeds, vegetables or meat with the garlic, then stir in the remaining ingredients along with the wine.

Creamy Tarragon
4 teaspoons Dijon mustard
½ cup heavy cream
2 tablespoons chopped fresh tarragon

Spiced Tomato
2 teaspoons fennel seeds
1 pound chopped heirloom tomatoes
¼ cup chopped fresh basil

Smoky Orange
3 ounces Spanish chorizo
½ cup halved pitted green olives
2 tablespoons grated orange zest

HOW TO CLEAN MUSSELS

Place the mussels in a colander. Under cold water, use a scrub brush to remove any sand, barnacles, mud, or seaweed. After scrubbing under cold water, remove the furry threads called the beard by grabbing them between your thumb and forefinger and pulling downward toward the hinged shell end (a paper towel can help you grip them).

2 tablespoons olive oil

1 large onion, chopped

2 medium carrots, cut into
¼-inch pieces

1 stalk celery, cut into ¼-inch pieces

1 small fennel bulb, cut into
¼-inch pieces

Kosher salt and pepper

2 large garlic cloves, finely chopped

6 thyme sprigs

½ cup dry white wine

1 28-ounce can whole peeled
tomatoes in juice

1 tablespoon chicken or vegetable
base (optional)

6 ounces orecchiette or other
short pasta

2 15-ounce cans white beans
(cannellini, navy, butter, or a
combination), rinsed

Chopped fresh flat-leaf parsley
and grated Parmesan cheese,
for topping

◀ Pasta e Fagioli

ACTIVE TIME 25 min. | **TOTAL TIME** 35 min. | **SERVES** 4-6

1. Heat the oil in a large Dutch oven on medium. Add the onion and cook, stirring occasionally, 5 minutes. Add the carrots, celery, fennel, ¾ teaspoon salt and ½ teaspoon pepper and cook, covered, stirring occasionally, until the vegetables are beginning to soften, 6 to 8 minutes more. Stir in the garlic and thyme and cook 2 minutes. Add the wine and simmer until nearly evaporated, 1 to 2 minutes.

2. Add the tomatoes and their juice, crushing them into small pieces as you add them to the pot. Add 5 cups water and the chicken base (if using) and bring to a boil. Add the pasta and simmer, stirring often, until barely tender, 8 to 12 minutes, depending on the type of pasta. Stir in the beans and cook until heated through, about 2 minutes. Remove the thyme and serve sprinkled with parsley and Parmesan.

PER SERVING *About 460 calories, 6.5 g fat (1.5 g saturated fat), 20 g protein, 820 mg sodium, 81 g carbohydrates, 18 g fiber*

TIP Add a Parmesan rind to your soup while it simmers for an extra cheesy kick (discard the rind before serving).

1 tablespoon olive oil

1 medium onion, chopped

3 cloves garlic, finely chopped

½ teaspoon salt

1 pound ground beef

1 28-ounce can crushed tomatoes

½ cup milk

3 tablespoons grated Pecorino cheese

1 8½-ounce package fully cooked
penne pasta, for serving

≡ QUICK & EASY ≡

Classic Bolognese Sauce

ACTIVE TIME 20 min. | **TOTAL TIME** 30 min. | **SERVES** 6

1. Heat the oil in a large saucepan. Add onion, garlic and ½ teaspoon salt and cook, stirring occasionally, for 10 minutes.

2. Add beef and cook, breaking it up with a spoon until no longer pink and beginning to brown, 5 to 6 minutes.

3. Stir in tomatoes, reduce heat and simmer for 10 minutes.

4. Stir in milk and Pecorino.

PER SERVING *About 575 calories, 21 g fat (7 g saturated fat), 27 g protein, 485 mg sodium, 70 g carbohydrates, 6 g fiber*

2 tablespoons olive oil

4 slices bacon, chopped

4 pounds lean beef brisket, trimmed and cut into 2-inch chunks

Kosher salt and pepper

3 small onions, cut into
½-inch-thick wedges

4 large carrots, cut into 2-inch pieces

6 garlic cloves, finely chopped

2 tablespoons tomato paste

2 tablespoons all-purpose flour

3 cups dry red wine

3 cups low-sodium beef broth

Thyme sprigs

2 bay leaves, optional

1 tablespoon unsalted butter

10 ounces small mushrooms, quartered

Chopped fresh flat-leaf parsley, for topping

Beef Bourguignon

ACTIVE TIME 50 min. | **TOTAL TIME** 3 hr. 50 min. | **SERVES** 8

1. Heat the oven to 375°F. Heat 1 tablespoon of the oil in a large Dutch oven on medium. Add the bacon and cook, stirring occasionally, until golden brown and crisp, about 5 minutes. Using a slotted spoon, transfer to a paper towel–lined plate. Discard all but 2 tablespoons of the fat in the pan.

2. Pat the beef dry with paper towels, season with ¾ teaspoon each salt and pepper, and cook in 3 batches, turning occasionally, until browned on all sides, 8 to 10 minutes total (adding additional oil to the pan as necessary).

3. Add the onions, season with ¼ teaspoon each salt and pepper, and cook, covered, stirring occasionally, 6 minutes. Add the carrots and cook, stirring occasionally, until the onions are just tender, 6 to 8 minutes more. Stir in two-thirds of the garlic and cook for 1 minute. Add the tomato paste and cook, stirring, 1 minute. Sprinkle the flour over the top and cook, stirring, for 2 minutes.

4. Stir in the wine. Return the beef and bacon to the pot, then add the broth, thyme and bay leaves; bring to a simmer. Cover, transfer the pot to the oven and cook until the beef is very tender and easily breaks apart, 3 to 3½ hours.

5. Five minutes before the beef is done, melt the butter in a large skillet on medium and add the remaining tablespoon oil. Add the mushrooms, season with ¼ teaspoon each salt and pepper, increase the heat to medium-high, and cook, tossing occasionally, for 6 minutes. Add the remaining garlic and cook, tossing, for 1 minute. Remove from the heat.

6. Discard the thyme and bay leaves from the stew, then fold in the mushrooms and sprinkle with parsley.

PER SERVING *About 440 calories, 20 g fat (7 g saturated fat), 52 g protein, 655 mg sodium, 14 g carbohydrates, 2 g fiber*

1 tablespoon olive oil

8 bone-in chicken thighs
(about 2¼ pounds)

Kosher salt and pepper

1 pound sweet Italian sausage
(about 5 links)

½ pound bacon, cut into
½-inch pieces

1 medium onion, finely chopped

2 medium carrots, finely chopped

1 stalk celery, finely chopped

2 cups fresh breadcrumbs
(about 5 ounces)

2 garlic cloves, pressed

2 tablespoons thyme leaves

2 15-ounce cans cannellini
beans, rinsed

2 cups low-sodium chicken broth

Chicken, Sausage & White Bean Stew

ACTIVE TIME 50 min. | **TOTAL TIME** 2 hr. 20 min. | **SERVES** 8

1. Heat the oven to 350°F. Heat the oil in a large Dutch oven on medium. Pat the chicken dry and season it with ¼ teaspoon each salt and pepper. Place the chicken skin side down in the pan. Cook until golden brown, about 6 minutes. Turn and cook for 3 minutes more. Transfer to a plate.

2. Add sausages to the pot and cook until browned all over, 6 to 8 minutes. Transfer to cutting board; let cool before slicing.

3. Add the bacon to the pot and cook, stirring occasionally, until golden brown and crisp, 8 to 10 minutes. With a slotted spoon, transfer to paper towels. Discard all but 2 tablespoons of the fat in the pot.

4. Add the onion and ¼ teaspoon salt to the pot and cook, stirring occasionally, until golden brown and tender, 5 to 6 minutes. Add the carrots and celery and cook for 3 minutes more. Remove from the heat.

5. In a small bowl, combine the breadcrumbs, garlic and thyme and set aside. Stir the beans and broth into the pot along with the chicken, sausage and bacon, and sprinkle with the breadcrumb mixture.

6. Bake until the chicken is fork-tender and the stew has thickened, about 1½ hours. Heat the broiler and broil until the crumbs are golden brown, about 3 minutes. Let stand 10 minutes before serving.

PER SERVING *About 535 calories, 29.5 g fat (9 g saturated fat), 35 g protein, 800 mg sodium, 31 g carbohydrates, 10 g fiber*

Chapter 3

The Sheet Pan & Casserole Dish

::

When it comes to foolproof family dinners, nothing is more forgiving than roasting, baking and broiling. These high-temperature techniques are hassle-free and hands-off. Even better, these methods develop great flavor and can be done in one versatile piece of equipment: a sheet pan or casserole dish.

What makes a good sheet pan?

A good sheet pan is hard to find. But we've got one—well, 30. We keep that many 18- by 12-inch baking sheets in the Test Kitchen. They're perfect for roasting and, with 1-inch-high sides, they allow for great browning but still catch pan juices. We prefer aluminum-coated steel or aluminum to nonstick pans. The surface of aluminum sheet pans ensures that vegetables, meats and sweets brown beautifully. It also doesn't scratch easily, which means it lasts longer. Given their versatility and longevity, sheet pans are a bargain, usually under $20 a piece. Sometimes labeled "half-sheet pans," they're available at many home supplies stores or online too.

What makes a good casserole dish?

Our favorite casserole dishes work hard. We prefer ones that are lightweight and have large handles that are easy to grasp when transferring the dish in and out of the oven. Our go-to size is about 2½ quarts and we like long, shallow rectangles that allow the food to cook quickly and evenly. We also suggest looking for a casserole dish that has a lid, which is helpful for storing food or keeping food warm when transporting.

TOP-TESTED SHEET PANS

In the Good Housekeeping Institute, we tested sheet pans for performance and ease of use. We made more than 200 cookies and roasted almost 20 pounds of broccoli to ensure even cooking in the oven, easy cleaning and no warping. We looked for sheet pans that are a cinch to clean, can handle repeated washing and can stand up to high heat.

BEST OVERALL
**Chicago Metallic Commerical II
Non-Stick Baking Sheet**
This sheet pan can't be beat for its performance, ease of use and affordable price. It bakes uniform cookies that slide right off the pan and provides consistently roasted vegetables. Plus, its nonstick coating makes it super easy to clean with little pressure needed.

**SCAN FOR MORE
SHEET PAN
LAB REVIEWS**

How to Choose a Sheet Pan

::::::::::::::::::::::::

Sheet pans are about as basic as you can get in terms of kitchen ware, but here are a few questions to think about before shopping for a new one.

Does the color make a difference?
Yes. Light colored sheet pans are your best bet for cooking foods evenly. Darker pans tend to absorb heat and lead to overcooking in less time. So go light—even if you choose a baking sheet with a nonstick finish.

How many do I need?
Invest in two sizes: Half-sheet pans are ideal for sheet pan dinners as well as for spreading out vegetables while roasting so they crisp up nicely on the outside (rather than steaming into mush in a crowded pan). Quarter-sheet pans are practically meant for one- or two-person cooking, whether you're making a protein or a side, and fit in many toaster ovens—plus, they're easier to clean than the larger pans.

Are there other tools to have on hand?
While a sheet pan is really all you need, adding the following items to your repertoire will make sheet pan cooking easier and more enjoyable.

Silicone cooking mats These help cut down on the use of parchment paper and make cleanup much easier.

Tongs Have tongs at the ready for turning foods halfway through cooking and transferring items to plates when finished.

Vegetable Roasting 101

You can roast just about anything, but vegetables especially benefit from the high, dry heat of the oven. Their flavor becomes concentrated, and their natural sugars caramelize, transforming them into richly satisfying sides. Refer to the chart below for tips on how to make perfectly crisp and caramelized vegetables every time.

As a general rule, for every 2 pounds of vegetables, add 1 tablespoon of olive oil and toss prior to roasting. Spread the vegetables on a sheet pan in a single layer, with space between the vegetables to allow heat to circulate around them. If the vegetables are overcrowded, they will steam rather than brown. You can roast different vegetables together if their cooking times are similar, so mix it up!

VEGETABLE ROASTING CHEAT SHEET

INGREDIENT	PREP	ROASTING TIME AT 450°F	FLAVORING
Asparagus	Trimmed	8–12 minutes	Sprinkle with lemon zest
Bell peppers	Cut into 1-inch-wide strips	15–25 minutes	Toss with chopped fresh parsley, a splash of vinegar and salt and pepper
Beets (without tops)	Whole, unpeeled, pricked with a fork, then peeled after roasting	1 hour	Salt, pepper and grated orange zest
Broccoli	Trimmed and stem peeled, split florets into ½-inch-wide pieces	10–15 minutes	Sprinkle with grated Parmesan or shredded extra-sharp Cheddar
Brussels sprouts	Trimmed and halved through the stem end	15–20 minutes	Toss with maple syrup immediately after roasting
Butternut squash	Peel, seed, and cut into 1-inch pieces	25–35 minutes	Toss with fresh thyme before roasting
Cauliflower	Cut into 1½-inch florets	20–30 minutes	Sprinkle with chopped fresh parsley and red pepper flakes
Green beans	Trimmed	10–15 minutes	Toss with chopped fresh dill, tarragon or chives
Potatoes and sweet potatoes	Cut into 1-inch-thick wedges	25–30 minutes	Toss with ground coriander or fresh rosemary before roasting

TOP-TESTED CASSEROLE DISHES

The Kitchen Appliances Lab tested eleven different casserole dishes, most of which were between 2½ and 3 quarts and 9 x 13-inch rectangular pans, an ideal size for making four- and six-serving meals. We tested boxed cornbread to assess evenness of browning on top and bottom, how long it took for casserole dishes to cool, nonstickability, the ease with which the dish could be transferred in and out of the oven, and how easy or difficult it was to clean. We also tested bread pudding to assess browning and cook time, as well as servability—could it handle metal utensils, did food stick?—and cleaning. Our favorite casserole dishes had minimal sticking, making them easy to serve from and easy to clean. We also liked oversized handles and lighter weight dishes, which made it easier to move them in and out of the oven.

BEST OVERALL
**Peugeot Appolia Rectangular
Baker Baking Pan**
The 13" Peugeot Appolia Baker scored the highest for ease of use and cleaning. It also made a nice, evenly cooked bread pudding. It took longer to cook than other casserole dishes we tested so we suggest increasing the cook time for more browning. It comes in an array of deep colors and sizes that nest inside of each other.

**SCAN FOR MORE
CASSEROLE DISH
LAB REVIEWS**

How to Choose a Casserole Dish

::::::::::::::::::::::::::

Casserole dishes are available in a wide variety of shapes, sizes, and materials like ceramic, glass, porcelain and even steel. Here are a few parameters to help you select the dish that's just right for you.

What size do I need?
When our Test Kitchen develops recipes, they most often reach for casserole dishes that are between 2½ and 3 quarts, because this size can most comfortably make four to six servings and they are easy to handle. Smaller sizes are great for side dishes, while larger sizes are perfect for entertaining or meal prep.

What shape do I need?
Casserole dishes come in all shapes from circles to squares. We find rectangles to be the most versatile in terms of what you can cook in them and how quickly. Generally, more surface area allows for quicker and more even heating.

What materials provide the best results?
When deciding which material is best for you, we recommend considering weight and cleanability first and foremost, though how well it browns food may be the most important factor for you.

Weight If you are looking for a lightweight casserole dish, consider glass, which tends to be lighter than ceramic, porcelain or steel and has the added bonus of allowing you to see all sides of a dish as it cooks.

Heat retention The cast iron casserole dish we tested was predictably heavy, but retained heat well, making it a great option for keeping foods warm longer.

Ease of cleaning Casserole dishes that are made of ceramic and coated with some sort of glaze are more durable and nonstick, making them easier to clean. These models are the best choice for those who don't want to deal with a lot of soaking and scrubbing.

Browning If browning is the most important factor to you, the best option is a lighter, coated carbon steel that heats quickly to allow for more even browning. Avoid glass casserole dishes, which did not brown as well as the other models we tested.

Freezer-to-oven safe? Some materials, like borosilicate glass and certain coated ceramics, can handle drastic changes in temperature, while most stoneware can't without cracking or shattering. Always check the manufacturer's instructions before attempting to use your dish in this way.

What other features should I look for?
The following other features can make casserole dishes easier to use, more versatile and convenient.

Handles Large, oversized handles are the easiest to grasp, especially with oven mitts.

Lids Some casserole dishes come with lids that can help keep food warm (particularly when made of the same, heavy-duty material as the casserole dish) or come in handy for storage.

Cooking Tips for Best Results

1. **Cut food into evenly sized pieces.** This general cooking rule remains true with sheet pan and casserole cooking. Uniform sized pieces will cook at the same rate, ensuring all parts of the meal are done at the same time.

2. **Toss vegetables in oil or seasonings.** Do this right on the sheet pan or in the casserole dish to cut down on excess dishes.

3. **Leave a little room between pieces of food.** This allows everything to cook evenly on all sides. Crowding pieces will lead to longer cooking times and food that is steamed instead of roasted.

4. **Account for cooking times.** When cooking vegetables and meats on the same sheet pan, place ingredients that take longer to cook (like potatoes) in the oven before adding items that cook in less time (like asparagus) to make sure all parts of the meal are done at the same time.

Garam Masala Roasted Chicken & Cauliflower

1 small head cauliflower (about 1½ pounds), quartered, cored, and cut into florets

3 tablespoons olive oil, divided

4 teaspoons garam masala, divided

1 red onion, cut into wedges

2 small jalapeños, sliced

Kosher salt and pepper

1 tablespoon brown sugar

¼ teaspoon cayenne

4 5-ounce boneless, skinless chicken breasts

Chopped fresh cilantro, for sprinkling

Lemon wedges, for serving (optional)

ACTIVE TIME 15 min. | **TOTAL TIME** 35 min. | **SERVES** 4

1. Heat oven to 450°F. On a rimmed baking sheet, toss the cauliflower with 2 tablespoons of the oil, then 2 teaspoons of the garam masala. Add the onion, jalapeños and ½ teaspoon each salt and pepper and toss to combine. Arrange in a single layer; roast for 10 minutes.

2. Meanwhile, in a medium bowl, combine the brown sugar, cayenne, remaining 1 tablespoon olive oil, remaining 2 teaspoons garam masala and ½ teaspoon each salt and pepper. Add the chicken and turn to coat.

3. Nestle the chicken among the vegetables, reduce the oven temperature to 400°F and roast until the chicken is cooked through and the vegetables are golden brown and tender, 15 to 20 minutes. Sprinkle with cilantro and serve with lemon wedges if desired.

PER SERVING About 290 calories, 13.5 g fat (2.5 g saturated), 30 g protein, 685 mg sodium, 11 g carbohydrates, 3 g fiber

Chicken Parmesan

3 tablespoons olive oil, divided

½ cup all-purpose flour

2 large eggs

1 teaspoon granulated garlic

Kosher salt

2 cups panko breadcrumbs

⅓ cup plus 2 tablespoons grated Parmesan cheese

4 5-ounce boneless, skinless chicken breasts, split, making 8 small cutlets

2 tablespoons fresh lemon juice

1 cup marinara sauce

4 ounces mozzarella cheese (do not use fresh), coarsely shredded

Chopped fresh flat-leaf parsley, for topping (optional)

ACTIVE TIME 25 min. | **TOTAL TIME** 55 min. | **SERVES** 4

1. Arrange oven racks so one is 6 inches from the broiler and heat the oven to 450°F. Rub a rimmed baking sheet with 1 tablespoon of the oil. Place the flour in a shallow bowl. In a second shallow bowl, beat together the eggs, garlic, 2 tablespoons water and ¾ teaspoon salt. In a third bowl, combine the panko with ⅓ cup of the Parmesan, then toss with the remaining 2 tablespoons oil.

2. In a fourth bowl, toss the chicken in the lemon juice. Dip each chicken breast in the flour, then the egg mixture (letting excess drip off), then the panko mixture, patting to help it adhere; transfer to the prepared baking sheet. Roast until the chicken is golden brown and cooked through, 12 to 18 minutes.

3. Heat the broiler. Spoon the marinara sauce over the chicken and sprinkle with the mozzarella and the remaining 2 tablespoons Parmesan. Broil on the top rack until the cheese has melted and turned golden brown in spots, 3 to 4 minutes. Sprinkle with parsley if desired.

PER SERVING About 635 calories, 25.5 g fat (8.5 g saturated), 48 g protein, 1,115 mg sodium, 51 g carbohydrates, 3 g fiber

Cornmeal, for baking sheet

Flour, for surface

1 pound pizza dough,
   at room temperature

4 ounces thinly sliced
   provolone cheese

3 ounces oyster mushrooms, trimmed,
   separated, any large mushrooms torn

3 ounces baby shiitake mushrooms,
   sliced ¼ inch thick

1 large shallot, sliced

2 tablespoons olive oil

Kosher salt and pepper

2 teaspoons fresh thyme leaves

½ cup ricotta cheese

½ cup grated Pecorino
   cheese, divided

1 teaspoon grated lemon zest

¼ to ½ teaspoon red pepper flakes

Chopped fresh flat-leaf parsley,
   for topping

⇒ QUICK & EASY ⇐

◄ Fall Mushroom Pizza

ACTIVE TIME 15 min. | **TOTAL TIME** 30 min. | **SERVES** 4

1. Heat the oven to 475°F. Sprinkle a baking sheet with cornmeal.

2. On a lightly floured surface, shape the pizza dough into a 14-inch circle or oval. Place on the prepared sheet and arrange the provolone on top.

3. In a large bowl, toss the mushrooms and shallot with the oil and ¼ teaspoon each salt and pepper, then fold in the thyme. Arrange the mushroom mixture on top of the provolone.

4. In the same bowl, combine the ricotta, ⅓ cup Pecorino, the lemon zest and ¼ teaspoon each salt and pepper. Dollop small spoonfuls over top of vegetables.

5. Sprinkle with red pepper flakes and the remaining Pecorino and bake until the crust is golden brown, 12 to 15 minutes. Sprinkle with parsley before serving.

PER SERVING *About 595 calories, 27 g fat (11.5 g saturated), 25 g protein, 1,715 mg sodium, 60 g carbohydrates, 4 g fiber*

Flour, for dusting

1 pound pizza dough, at
   room temperature

Cornmeal, for baking sheet (optional)

½ ounce extra-sharp Cheddar,
   coarsely shredded

1 small onion, thinly sliced

1 small red bell pepper, sliced

1 small yellow bell pepper, sliced

1 poblano pepper, halved and
   thinly sliced

1 small jalapeño, halved and
   thinly sliced

1 tablespoon olive oil

Kosher salt and pepper

⇒ QUICK & EASY ⇐

Hot Pepper & Onion Pizza

ACTIVE TIME 15 min. | **TOTAL TIME** 30 min. | **SERVES** 4

1. Heat the oven to 500°F (if you can't heat your oven this high without broiling, heat to 475°F).

2. On a lightly floured surface, shape the pizza dough into a 14-inch oval. Place on a cornmeal-dusted or parchment-lined baking sheet. Sprinkle the Cheddar over the top.

3. In a large bowl, toss the onion, peppers and jalapeño with the olive oil and ¼ teaspoon each salt and pepper. Scatter over the dough and bake until the crust is golden brown, 10 to 12 minutes.

PER SERVING *About 330 calories, 6.5 g fat (1.5 g saturated fat), 12 g protein, 690 mg sodium, 57 g carbohydrates, 3 g fiber*

1½ pounds skin-on salmon fillet

2 tablespoons olive oil, divided

Kosher salt and pepper

2 tablespoons everything spice blend

1 lemon

1 small fennel bulb, cored and very thinly sliced, plus ½ cup fronds

3 scallions, thinly sliced

½ cup flat-leaf parsley leaves

½ cup cilantro leaves

‹ Everything Bagel Crusted Salmon

ACTIVE TIME 20 min. | **TOTAL TIME** 25 min. | **SERVES** 4

1. Heat the oven to 425°F. Place the salmon, skin side down, on a rimmed baking sheet and rub with 1 tablespoon of the oil, then sprinkle ¼ teaspoon pepper and the everything spice on top. Thinly slice half of the lemon and arrange around the salmon. Bake until the salmon is barely opaque throughout, 18 to 22 minutes.

2. Meanwhile, squeeze the juice from the remaining lemon half (about 1½ tablespoons) into a medium bowl. Add the fennel, the remaining tablespoon oil and ¼ teaspoon each salt and pepper and toss to coat.

3. Just before serving, toss the fennel with the scallions, parsley, cilantro and fennel fronds. Serve with the salmon and lemon slices.

PER SERVING *About 300 calories, 14 g fat (2.5 g saturated fat), 37 g protein, 330 mg sodium, 8 g carbohydrates, 3 g fiber*

6 garlic cloves, smashed

1¼ pounds green beans, trimmed

1 pint grape tomatoes

½ cup pitted Kalamata olives

3 anchovy fillets, chopped (optional)

2 tablespoons olive oil

Kosher salt and pepper

1¼ pounds skinless salmon fillet, cut into 4 pieces

Greek yogurt, for serving (optional)

Salmon with Roasted Green Beans & Tomatoes

ACTIVE TIME 5 min. | **TOTAL TIME** 20 min. | **SERVES** 4

1. Heat the oven to 425°F. On a rimmed baking sheet, toss the garlic, green beans, tomatoes, olives and anchovies (if using) with 1 tablespoon of the oil and ¼ teaspoon pepper. Roast until the vegetables are tender and beginning to brown, 12 to 15 minutes.

2. Meanwhile, heat the remaining tablespoon oil in a large skillet on medium. Season salmon with ¼ teaspoon each salt and pepper and cook until golden brown and opaque throughout, 4 to 5 minutes per side. Serve with the vegetables and yogurt if desired.

PER SERVING *About 330 calories, 15 g fat (3 g saturated fat), 31 g protein, 445 mg sodium, 15 g carbohydrates, 5 g fiber*

1½ pounds large shrimp, peeled and deveined

1 12-ounce jar roasted red peppers, drained and cut into 1-inch pieces

4 scallions, sliced

2 garlic cloves, pressed

2 tablespoons dry white wine

1 tablespoon lemon juice

Kosher salt and pepper

2 tablespoons olive oil

4 ounces feta cheese, crumbled

Pitas and baby spinach, cooked rice or couscous, or salad greens, for serving

‹ Roasted Garlicky Shrimp

ACTIVE TIME 10 min. | **TOTAL TIME** 25 min. | **SERVES** 4

1. Heat the oven to 425°F. In a 1½- to 2-quart baking dish, combine the shrimp, red peppers, scallions, garlic, wine, lemon juice and ¼ teaspoon each salt and pepper.

2. Drizzle with the olive oil and sprinkle with the feta. Bake until the shrimp are opaque throughout, 12 to 15 minutes. Spoon into pitas along with baby spinach, serve over rice or couscous or toss with your favorite salad greens.

PER SERVING *About 285 calories, 14.5 g fat (5.5 g saturated fat), 28 g protein, 1,465 mg sodium, 9 g carbohydrates, 3 g fiber*

1½ pounds spiralized zucchini

2 tablespoons olive oil

Kosher salt and pepper

20 large shrimp, peeled and deveined

4 scallions, thinly sliced

4 garlic cloves, thinly sliced

1 small red chile, thinly sliced

2 tablespoons dry white wine

1 tablespoon lemon juice

4 ounces feta cheese, crumbled

Roasted Shrimp Scampi & Zoodles

ACTIVE TIME 25 min. | **TOTAL TIME** 25 min. | **SERVES** 4

1. Heat the oven to 475°F. On a rimmed baking sheet, toss the zucchini with 1 tablespoon of the oil and ¼ teaspoon each salt and pepper; arrange in an even layer and roast for 6 minutes.

2. Meanwhile, in a bowl, toss the shrimp, scallions, garlic and chile with the wine, lemon juice and ¼ teaspoon each salt and pepper.

3. Scatter the shrimp over the zucchini, drizzle with the remaining tablespoon oil and sprinkle with the feta. Roast until the shrimp are opaque throughout, 5 to 7 minutes.

PER SERVING *About 200 calories, 13.5 g fat (5.5 g saturated fat), 11 g protein, 715 mg sodium, 10 g carbohydrates, 2 g fiber*

Sheet Pan Chickpea Chicken

ACTIVE TIME 5 min. | **TOTAL TIME** 35 min. | **SERVES** 4

1 15½-ounce can chickpeas, rinsed

1 16-ounce bag mini sweet peppers, cored and chopped

2 tablespoons olive oil

Kosher salt and pepper

2 tablespoons harissa sauce

4 small skin-on chicken legs (about 2½ pounds)

Chopped fresh cilantro, for topping

1. Heat the oven to 425°F. On a rimmed baking sheet, toss the chickpeas and peppers with 1 tablespoon of the oil and ¼ teaspoon each salt and pepper.

2. In a small bowl, whisk together the harissa and the remaining tablespoon oil. Rub the chicken with the harissa mixture. Nestle the chicken among the chickpeas and peppers and roast until the chicken is golden brown and cooked through, 20 to 25 minutes.

3. Toss with cilantro before serving.

PER SERVING *About 630 calories, 42 g fat (10 g saturated fat), 39 g protein, 600 mg sodium, 22 g carbohydrates, 6 g fiber*

TIP **Shred any leftover chicken, discarding the skin and bones. Thinly slice any leftover peppers. Toss the chicken and peppers with the chickpeas and refrigerate for up to 3 days. Spread pita bread with Greek yogurt and fill with the chicken mixture and baby arugula for a delicious lunch.**

≡ QUICK & EASY ≡

Mint & Feta Mini Meatloaves

ACTIVE TIME 10 min. | **TOTAL TIME** 30 min. | **SERVES** 4

1¼ pounds ground beef chuck

½ cup crumbled feta cheese

½ cup finely chopped fresh mint

Kosher salt

1 large leek, sliced

3 medium yellow squash, chopped

1 cup pitted green olives

1 tablespoon olive oil

1. Heat the oven to 450°F.

2. Combine the ground beef, feta, mint and ¼ teaspoon salt. Form the mixture into 4 mini loaves on a baking sheet.

3. In a bowl, toss the leek, yellow squash and green olives with the olive oil and ⅛ teaspoon salt. Arrange the vegetables around the meatloaves on the baking sheet. Roast for 15 to 20 minutes or until meatloaves are cooked through (165°F).

PER SERVING *About 415 calories, 28 g fat (10 g saturated fat), 30 g protein, 935 mg sodium, 12 g carbohydrates, 4 g fiber*

Flour, for surface

1 pound pizza dough, at room temperature

Cornmeal, for baking sheet (optional)

1½ tablespoons Dijon mustard

4 ounces thinly sliced provolone cheese

1 small yellow onion, thinly sliced

1 small red onion, thinly sliced

1 small fennel bulb, cored and thinly sliced

1½ tablespoons olive oil

2 teaspoons fresh thyme leaves

Kosher salt and pepper

2 ounces Fontina cheese, coarsely shredded

Finely chopped fresh flat-leaf parsley, for topping

‹ Onion Flatbread

ACTIVE TIME 15 min. | **TOTAL TIME** 30 min. | **SERVES** 4-6

1. Heat oven to 500°F (if you can't heat the oven this high without broiling, heat to 475°F).

2. On a lightly floured surface, shape the pizza dough into a 14-inch oval. Place on a cornmeal-dusted or parchment-lined baking sheet. Spread with the mustard, then top with the provolone.

3. In a large bowl, toss the onions, fennel, oil, thyme and ½ teaspoon each salt and pepper; fold in the Fontina. Scatter over the dough and bake until the crust is golden brown and the vegetables are just tender, 10 to 12 minutes. Sprinkle with parsley before serving.

PER SERVING *About 400 calories, 16 g fat (6.5 g saturated), 14 g protein, 1,310 mg sodium, 46 g carbohydrates, 3 g fiber*

Cornmeal, for surface

1 pound pizza dough

½ medium head cauliflower (about 1 pound), thinly sliced

1 small red onion, thinly sliced

½ cup chopped fresh flat-leaf parsley

2 tablespoons olive oil

¼ teaspoon red pepper flakes (optional)

Kosher salt

4 ounces Gruyère cheese, coarsely shredded (about 1¾ cups)

Roasted Cauliflower Pizza

ACTIVE TIME 15 min. | **TOTAL TIME** 40 min. | **SERVES** 4

1. Heat the oven to 425°F. Dust a baking sheet with cornmeal. Shape the pizza dough into a 16-inch oval and place on the prepared sheet.

2. In a large bowl, toss the cauliflower, onion and parsley with the olive oil, red pepper flakes if using and ½ teaspoon salt. Fold in the Gruyère.

3. Scatter the vegetable mixture over the dough. Bake until the cauliflower is tender and the crust is golden brown and crisp, 20 to 25 minutes.

PER SERVING *About 337 calories, 16 g fat (6 g saturated fat), 15 g protein, 741 mg sodium, 32 g carbohydrates, 1.5 g fiber*

2 large bell peppers (1 red and
   1 orange), sliced

1 fennel bulb, cored and sliced

1 medium onion, cut into wedges

4 tablespoons olive oil, divided

Kosher salt and pepper

1¼ pounds cod or halibut fillet

3 tablespoons sherry vinegar

3 tablespoons capers, drained
   and chopped

1 tablespoon anchovy paste

1 garlic clove, grated

½ cup finely chopped fresh
   flat-leaf parsley

◄ Sheet Pan Fish & Vegetables

ACTIVE TIME 15 min. | **TOTAL TIME** 25 min. | **SERVES** 4

1. Heat the oven to 450°F. On a rimmed baking sheet, toss the peppers, fennel and onion with 2 tablespoons oil and ½ teaspoon each salt and pepper. Roast for 15 minutes.

2. Reduce the oven temp to 425°F; toss the vegetables, then nestle the fish among them. Season with ¼ teaspoon each salt and pepper and continue roasting until the fish is opaque throughout, 10 to 12 minutes more.

3. Meanwhile, in a small bowl, combine the vinegar, capers, anchovy paste, garlic, remaining 2 tablespoons oil and ¼ teaspoon salt; stir in the parsley. Serve spooned over fish.

PER SERVING *About 295 calories, 15.5 g fat (2 g saturated fat), 26 g protein, 895 mg sodium, 14 g carbohydrates, 4 g fiber*

TIP A 1¼-pound piece of cod or halibut easily feeds four.

---

1 pound small yellow potatoes
   (about 16), halved lengthwise

2 small red onions, cut into
   ½-inch-thick wedges

4 slices bacon, cut into ½-inch pieces

1 tablespoon mayonnaise

1 tablespoon Dijon mustard

1 teaspoon finely grated lemon zest

¼ cup panko breadcrumbs

1 tablespoon olive oil

1 tablespoon thyme leaves

4 6-ounce pieces cod fillet
   (at least 1 inch thick)

Black pepper

Fish Chowder Sheet Pan Bake

ACTIVE TIME 15 min. | **TOTAL TIME** 15 min. | **SERVES** 4

1. Heat the oven to 450°F. Pile the potatoes and onions in the center of a rimmed baking sheet and place the bacon on top. Roast for 10 minutes.

2. Meanwhile, in a small bowl, combine the mayonnaise, mustard and lemon zest. In a second small bowl, combine the panko with the oil, then fold in the thyme. Season the fish with ½ teaspoon pepper, then spread with the mayonnaise mixture and sprinkle with the panko.

3. Remove the baking sheet from the oven and reduce oven temperature to 425°F. Toss the potato and onion mixture together, then spread out in an even layer, arranging the potatoes cut side down.

4. Nestle the fish pieces among the vegetables and roast until the fish is opaque throughout and the potatoes are golden brown and tender, 12 to 15 minutes.

PER SERVING *About 412 calories, 18 g fat (5 g saturated fat), 33 g protein, 435 mg sodium, 28 g carbohydrates, 3 g fiber*

4 garlic cloves, pressed

1 large shallot, finely chopped

1 cup chopped fresh flat-leaf parsley

2 tablespoons finely chopped
  fresh rosemary

1 tablespoon grated orange zest

4 tablespoons olive oil, divided

Kosher salt and pepper

2 skin-on boneless turkey breast
  halves (about 2 pounds total)

Fresh herbs, for topping (optional)

Grapes and gravy, for serving
  (optional)

Turkey Roulade

ACTIVE TIME 45 min. | **TOTAL TIME** 1 hr. 15 min. | **SERVES** 8

1. Heat the oven to 425°F. In a medium bowl, combine the garlic, shallot, parsley, rosemary, orange zest, 2 tablespoons olive oil and ½ teaspoon each salt and pepper.

2. Working with 1 turkey breast half at a time, remove the skin in one piece, being careful not to tear it and set aside.

3. Butterfly and pound each breast to ¼ inch thick. Divide the herb mixture between the breasts, leaving a ¾-inch border all the way around. Starting at short end, roll up each turkey breast. Lay the skin on top of each breast, tucking and wrapping under the edges, then tie with kitchen string, spacing about 2 inches apart. Transfer to a rimmed baking sheet. (For step-by-step instructions, see How to Stuff a Turkey Breast below.)

4. Brush each breast with 1 tablespoon oil, season with ½ teaspoon salt and roast for 25 minutes. Reduce the oven temp to 375°F and continue roasting until the internal temperature reaches 160°F on an instant-read thermometer, 25 to 30 minutes more. Transfer the breasts to a cutting board and let rest for at least 10 minutes.

5. Remove the string, slice the turkey and arrange on platter. Garnish with fresh herbs and grapes, and serve with your favorite gravy if desired.

PER SERVING *About 240 calories, 13.5 g fat (3 g saturated fat), 26 g protein, 300 mg sodium, 2 g carbohydrates, 1 g fiber*

HOW TO STUFF A TURKEY BREAST

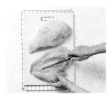

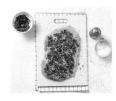

1. Using a sharp knife, butterfly the breast, starting from the side and cutting nearly all the way through, then open it like a book.

2. Place plastic over the breast and pound to ¼ inch thick.

3. Spread herb mixture over the breast meat, leaving a ¾-inch border all the way around.

4. Starting at the short end, roll up the turkey breast.

5. Lay the skin on top of the breast, tucking and wrapping it under the edges, then tie with kitchen string about 2 inches apart.

2 fennel bulbs, cored and sliced into ¼-inch pieces

1 tablespoon olive oil

Kosher salt and pepper

1 navel orange

2 tablespoons honey

2 tablespoons grated peeled fresh ginger

2 teaspoons fennel seeds, coarsely crushed

1 4- to 5-pound chicken, giblets discarded

1 pound mixed mushrooms, cut if large

1 tablespoon sherry vinegar

1 small head radicchio, torn into large pieces

Chopped fresh flat-leaf parsley, for topping (optional)

Orange-Ginger Roast Chicken with Fennel & Radicchio Salad

ACTIVE TIME 10 min. | **TOTAL TIME** 1 hr. 30 min. | **SERVES** 8

1. Heat the oven to 350°F. Line a rimmed baking sheet with parchment paper. On the prepared baking sheet, toss the fennel with the oil and ½ teaspoon each salt and pepper. Move to outer edges of pan.

2. Grate the zest of the orange into a small bowl, then squeeze in 3 tablespoons juice (reserve the orange halves). Whisk in the honey to dissolve, then stir in the ginger and fennel seeds.

3. Pat the chicken dry, place in the center of the prepared baking sheet and stuff with the orange halves, then brush with half of the juice mixture. Roast for 40 minutes.

4. Increase the oven temp to 425°F. Toss the mushrooms with the fennel and brush the chicken with remaining juice mixture. Roast until the temperature reaches 165°F on an instant-read thermometer inserted into thickest part of chicken thigh, 25 to 30 minutes. Transfer the chicken to a cutting board and let rest at least 10 minutes before carving.

5. Toss the mushrooms and fennel with the vinegar, season with salt and pepper if necessary and then fold in radicchio. Serve the vegetables with the chicken, topped with parsley if desired.

PER SERVING *About 345 calories, 18.5 g fat (5 g saturated fat), 32 g protein, 245 mg sodium, 13 g carbohydrates, 3 g fiber*

2 tablespoons olive oil

1 tablespoon lime juice, plus lime wedges for serving

½ teaspoon honey

1 tablespoon tomato paste

1 teaspoon chili powder

½ teaspoon ground coriander

½ teaspoon ground cumin

⅛ teaspoon cayenne

Kosher salt

1 medium cauliflower, cored and cut into small florets

8 small tortillas, charred

Spicy Taco Slaw, below

Lime wedges and chopped fresh cilantro, for serving

‹ Roasted Cauliflower Tacos

ACTIVE TIME 10 min. | **TOTAL TIME** 25 min. | **SERVES** 4

1. Heat the oven to 425°F. In a large bowl, whisk together the oil, lime juice and honey. Whisk in the tomato paste, chili powder, coriander, cumin, cayenne and ½ teaspoon salt.

2. Add the cauliflower and toss to coat. Arrange on a rimmed baking sheet and roast until golden brown and tender, 18 to 22 minutes.

3. Spoon the cauliflower into tortillas and top with slaw. Serve with lime wedges and cilantro.

PER SERVING *About 360 calories, 16.5 g fat (3.5 g saturated fat), 10 g protein, 1,165 mg sodium, 46 g carbohydrates, 7 g fiber*

2 tablespoons lime juice

1 to 2 tablespoons regular or vegan mayonnaise

Kosher salt

¼ small head purple cabbage, cored and very thinly sliced

1 small red bell pepper, quartered and thinly sliced

1 small jalapeño, thinly sliced

¼ cup roughly chopped fresh cilantro

Spicy Taco Slaw

ACTIVE TIME 15 min. | **TOTAL TIME** 15 min. | **SERVES** 4

In a large bowl, whisk together the lime juice, 1 tablespoon mayonnaise and ½ teaspoon salt. Add cabbage and toss to coat, adding more mayo if desired. Toss with the bell pepper and jalapeño. Fold in the cilantro just before serving.

PER SERVING *About 60 calories, 4.5 g fat (0.5 g saturated fat), 1 g protein, 280 mg sodium, 4 g carbohydrates, 1 g fiber*

2 tablespoons lemon juice

1½ to 2 tablespoons gochujang
(Korean hot pepper paste)

1 tablespoon olive oil

2 teaspoons honey

2 teaspoons grated peeled
fresh ginger

1 garlic clove, grated

1½ pounds large shrimp, peeled
and deveined

1 head Boston lettuce,
leaves separated

2 Persian cucumbers, sliced

1 bunch small radishes, sliced

Fresh mint and basil, chopped,
for topping

‹ Spicy Shrimp Lettuce Wraps

ACTIVE TIME 20 min. | **TOTAL TIME** 25 min. | **SERVES** 1

1. Heat the oven to 425°F. In a large bowl, whisk together the lemon juice, gochujang, oil and honey, then stir in the ginger and garlic. Add the shrimp and toss to coat.

2. Arrange the shrimp in a single layer on a rimmed baking sheet and roast until they are just opaque throughout, 10 to 15 minutes.

3. Serve the shrimp in lettuce cups and top with cucumbers, radishes, mint and basil.

PER SERVING *About 230 calories, 4.5 g fat (0.5 g saturated fat), 36 g protein, 705 mg sodium, 13 g carbohydrates, 1 g fiber*

TIP Gochujang will amp up the flavor of any dish. It's a fermented paste made with gochugaru, a Korean red pepper, and a blend of flours. It adds a spicy kick, along with mild sweetness, to marinades and sauces. Note: Each brand has different levels of spice, so be sure to taste a little bit before adding it to your meal so you don't accidentally go too heavy on the heat.

1½ pounds small boneless, skinless
chicken breasts

Kosher salt and pepper

8 thin slices pancetta

1 pound green beans, trimmed

2 tablespoons olive oil

Lemon wedges, for serving

Pancetta Chicken

ACTIVE TIME 15 min. | **TOTAL TIME** 30 min. | **SERVES** 4

1. Heat the oven to 450°F. Line a rimmed baking sheet with aluminum foil.

2. Sprinkle the chicken with ½ teaspoon salt. Drape 2 slices of pancetta over each piece of chicken and tuck the ends underneath to wrap; place on prepared sheet. Transfer to the oven and roast for 12 minutes.

3. In a bowl, toss the green beans with the olive oil and season with salt and pepper. Scatter the beans around the chicken and roast until the chicken is cooked through and the green beans are golden brown and tender, 10 to 12 minutes more. Serve with lemon wedges.

PER SERVING *About 265 calories, 8 g fat (2 g saturated fat), 38 g protein, 520 mg sodium, 10 g carbohydrates, 4 g fiber*

6 ounces tortilla chips (about 7 cups)

1 15-ounce can low-sodium black
  beans, rinsed

8 ounces extra-sharp Cheddar cheese,
  coarsely shredded (about 2 cups)

1 15-ounce can refried beans

¼ cup sour cream

1 cup shredded romaine lettuce

½ cup fresh pico de gallo

½ cup guacamole

◂ Double Bean Nachos

ACTIVE TIME 15 min. | **TOTAL TIME** 15 min. | **SERVES** 6

1. Heat the oven to 450°F. On a rimmed baking sheet, toss the chips, black beans and half the Cheddar.

2. Dollop refried beans on top and sprinkle with the remaining Cheddar. Bake until the beans are heated through and the cheese has melted, 6 to 7 minutes.

3. Dollop sour cream over the nachos and top with the lettuce, pico de gallo and guacamole.

PER SERVING *About 450 calories, 25 g fat (9 g saturated fat), 19.5 g protein, 760 mg sodium, 42 g carbohydrates, 10 g fiber*

TIP Tossing chips, beans and half the cheese before arranging on a sheet pan and then topping with more delicate items such as refried beans and more cheese ensures each bite will have the perfect ratio of chip to topping. When they are out of the oven, add other toppings such as sour cream, guac or salsa (or all three!).

---

4 large eggs

¼ cup half-and-half or milk

Kosher salt

1 cup shredded Mexican cheese blend

1 cup crumbled goat cheese

¼ cup finely chopped fresh cilantro

2 cups thinly sliced kale

1½ cups chopped tomatoes

½ cup corn kernels

4 cups tortilla chips

Tex-Mex Tortilla Casserole

ACTIVE TIME 10 min. | **TOTAL TIME** 45 min. | **SERVES** 6

1. Heat the oven to 400°F. Make the egg base: Whisk the eggs, half-and-half and ½ teaspoon salt. Stir in the shredded cheese, goat cheese and cilantro.

2. In a large bowl, combine the egg base with the kale, tomatoes, corn and tortilla chips. Toss to coat.

3. Add the mixture to a 2- to 2½-quart baking dish. Cover and bake 30 to 35 minutes or until the egg sets and the cheese melts. Uncover for the last 5 minutes to brown the top.

PER SERVING *About 415 calories, 12 g fat (3 g saturated fat), 15 g protein, 215 mg sodium, 65 g carbohydrates, 5 g fiber*

1 tablespoon fennel seeds

1 tablespoon finely grated orange zest

3 bell peppers (red, yellow, and orange), cut into 1-inch chunks

3 garlic cloves, thinly sliced

3 tablespoons olive oil

Kosher salt and pepper

4 small chicken legs (about 2 pounds)

4 cups baby spinach

2 ounces feta cheese, crumbled

≡ QUICK & EASY ≡

‹ Fennel Roasted Chicken & Peppers

ACTIVE TIME 15 min. | **TOTAL TIME** 45 min. | **SERVES** 4

1. Heat the oven to 425°F. In a small skillet, toast the fennel seeds and orange zest until lightly browned and fragrant, 3 to 4 minutes. Transfer to spice grinder or blender and pulse to blend and grind. Set aside.

2. On a rimmed baking sheet, toss the peppers and garlic with 2 tablespoons of the oil and ½ teaspoon each salt and pepper and arrange in an even layer.

3. Rub the chicken legs with the remaining tablespoon oil, then with the fennel-orange mixture. Nestle the chicken among the vegetables on the baking sheet and roast until it is golden brown and cooked through and peppers are tender, 25 to 30 minutes.

4. Transfer the chicken to plates, scatter spinach over the peppers remaining on the sheet and toss until just beginning to wilt. Sprinkle the vegetables with the feta and serve with the chicken.

PER SERVING *About 530 calories, 40 g fat (11 g saturated fat), 32 g protein, 495 mg sodium, 11 g carbohydrates, 3 g fiber*

2 medium-size red onions, cut into 8 wedges

1½ pounds medium carrots, quartered lengthwise

½ pound medium parsnips, quartered lengthwise

3 tablespoons olive oil, divided

Kosher salt and ground black pepper

2 tablespoons pink peppercorns

1 tablespoon green peppercorns

1 tablespoon black peppercorns

1½ tablespoons finely chopped fresh rosemary

2 teaspoons honey

1 3½-pound trimmed beef tenderloin, tied with string

Rosemary Beef Tenderloin with Root Vegetables

ACTIVE TIME 25 min. | **TOTAL TIME** 1 hr. | **SERVES** 8

1. Heat the oven to 425°F with oven racks in upper and lower thirds. Toss together the onions, carrots, parsnips and 2 tablespoons of the oil on a rimmed baking sheet. Season with salt and ground pepper. Transfer half of the vegetables to a second baking sheet.

2. Using the bottom of a heavy pan, coarsely crush the pink, green and black peppercorns; transfer to a bowl. Add the rosemary, honey and remaining tablespoon oil and stir to combine. Season with salt. Rub over the beef and nestle the beef among the vegetables on one of the baking sheets.

3. Roast both baking sheets, with the beef on the top rack, 15 minutes. Rotate pans and roast until an instant-read thermometer inserted into the thickest part of the beef registers 125°F for medium-rare, 14 to 16 minutes. Transfer the beef to a cutting board and loosely tent with aluminum foil; let rest 20 minutes before slicing. Serve with the vegetables.

PER SERVING *About 585 calories, 41 g fat (15 g saturated fat), 36 g protein, 395 mg sodium, 17 g carbohydrates, 5 g fiber*

Oil, for pan

4 ounces cream cheese,
   at room temperature

⅓ cup red enchilada sauce

¼ cup sour cream

Kosher salt and pepper

3 cups finely shredded white-meat
   rotisserie chicken

6 ounces colby jack cheese,
   coarsely shredded

½ cup chopped fresh cilantro

12 small corn tortillas

Olive oil, for brushing

Pico de gallo, sour cream and
   crumbled cotija cheese, for serving

‹ Chicken Taquitos

ACTIVE TIME 30 min. | **TOTAL TIME** 30 min. | **SERVES** 4-6

1. Heat the oven to 425°F and brush a rimmed baking sheet with oil.

2. In a large bowl, combine the cream cheese, enchilada sauce, sour cream and ½ teaspoon each salt and pepper. Fold in chicken, colby jack and cilantro.

3. In batches, place tortillas on microwave-safe plate and cover with damp paper towel. Microwave until warm and pliable, 30 to 60 seconds.

4. Divide mixture among tortillas (scant ¼ cup each), roll up tightly, and place on the prepared baking sheet, seam sides down. Brush with oil and bake until golden brown and crisp, 12 to 15 minutes.

5. Transfer to platter and serve with pico de gallo, sour cream and cotija.

PER SERVING *About 405 calories, 21.5 g fat (11.5 g saturated fat), 29 g protein, 705 mg sodium, 21 g carbohydrates, 3 g fiber*

TIP Craving a little extra crunch? Instead of baking, air fry at 400°F for 8 to 10 minutes.

1 10-ounce container low-sodium
   cottage cheese

1 10-ounce package frozen leaf
   spinach, thawed and squeezed of
   excess moisture

3 ounces part-skim mozzarella cheese,
   coarsely shredded (about ¾ cup)

4 tablespoons grated Pecorino
   cheese, divided

⅛ teaspoon freshly grated nutmeg

Kosher salt and pepper

1 10-ounce package frozen squash
   puree, thawed

8 no-boil lasagna noodles

½ cup crème fraîche

1 tablespoon water

Winter Squash & Spinach Lasagna

ACTIVE TIME 10 min. | **TOTAL TIME** 55 min. | **SERVES** 1

1. Heat the oven to 425°F. In a food processor, puree the cottage cheese and spinach until smooth. Transfer to a bowl and fold in ½ cup of the mozzarella, 2 tablespoons of the Pecorino, the nutmeg, ½ teaspoon salt and ¼ teaspoon pepper.

2. Spread ½ cup of the squash on the bottom of an 8-inch square baking dish. Top with 2 noodles and spread a third (about ¼ cup) of the remaining squash over the top. Dollop with a third (about ¾ cup) of the cottage cheese mixture; repeat twice.

3. Place the remaining 2 noodles on top. In a small bowl, combine the crème fraîche and water and spread over the top of the noodles. Sprinkle with the remaining ¼ cup mozzarella and the remaining 2 tablespoons Pecorino.

4. Cover tightly with an oiled piece of foil (to prevent sticking) and bake 15 minutes. Uncover and bake until the noodles are tender and the top is golden brown, 8 to 10 minutes more. For deep golden brown, broil for 2 minutes.

PER SERVING *About 460 calories, 19.5 g fat (11.5 g saturated fat), 26 g protein, 585 mg sodium, 45 g carbohydrates, 5 g fiber*

1 pound ground pork

2 scallions, finely chopped

1 tablespoon grated peeled
 fresh ginger

Kosher salt and pepper

1/2 cup sweet chili sauce (we used
 Mae Ploy)

1/2 seedless cucumber

1 baguette

Mayonnaise, chopped fresh mint and
 cilantro, and thinly sliced red chile,
 for serving

‹ Gingery Pork Meatball Subs

ACTIVE TIME 10 min. | **TOTAL TIME** 20 min. | **SERVES** 4

1. Heat the oven to 450°F. In a large bowl, combine pork, scallions, ginger and 1/2 teaspoon each salt and pepper. Drop 16 spoonfuls (about 2 tablespoons) pork mixture onto a rimmed baking sheet and roast until browned and cooked through, 8 to 10 minutes. Transfer to a bowl and toss with chili sauce.

2. Meanwhile, cut cucumber into matchsticks. Cut baguette crosswise into 4 pieces, then split each piece. Spread bread with mayonnaise and fill with meatballs, cucumber, mint, cilantro and chile.

PER SERVING *About 585 calories, 26.5 g fat (6.5 g saturated fat), 28 g protein, 1,040 mg sodium, 51 g carbohydrates, 3 g fiber*

---

1 15-ounce container part-skim
 ricotta cheese

1/4 cup plus 2 tablespoons grated
 Pecorino, divided

Kosher salt and pepper

4 cups baby spinach, roughly chopped

4 ounces part-skim mozzarella cheese,
 coarsely shredded, divided

1/2 cup flat-leaf parsley,
 roughly chopped

2 cups marinara sauce or Classic
 Bolognese Sauce (page 45)

6 no-boil lasagna noodles

Classic Lasagna

ACTIVE TIME 30 min. | **TOTAL TIME** 1 hr. | **SERVES** 4

1. Heat the oven to 425°F.

2. In a bowl, combine the ricotta, 1/4 cup of the Pecorino and 1/4 teaspoon each salt and pepper. Fold in the spinach, all but 1/2 cup of the mozzarella and the remaining 1/2 cup parsley.

3. Spread 1/2 cup sauce on the bottom of an 8-inch square baking dish. Top with 2 noodles and spread one-third (about 1/4 cup) of the remaining sauce over the top. Dollop with one-third (about 1 cup) of the ricotta mixture; repeat. Place the remaining 2 noodles on top; spread with the remaining sauce and dollop with the remaining ricotta mixture.

4. Sprinkle with the remaining 1/2 cup mozzarella and 2 tablespoons Pecorino, cover tightly with an oiled piece of foil (to prevent sticking), and bake 15 minutes. Uncover and bake until the noodles are tender and the top is golden brown, 8 to 10 minutes more.

PER SERVING *About 613 calories, 29 g fat (12 g saturated fat), 51 g protein, 824 mg sodium, 38 g carbohydrates, 3 g fiber*

Mini Meatballs with Garlicky Tomatoes

1 3-inch piece baguette
(about 1 ounce)

2 large eggs

4 garlic cloves (2 finely chopped,
2 pressed)

2 cups packed baby spinach (1 cup
finely chopped, 1 cup finely sliced)

¼ cup finely grated Parmesan cheese

½ teaspoon dried oregano

Kosher salt and pepper

1 pound ground beef

1 pound Campari tomatoes

1 tablespoon olive oil

ACTIVE TIME 45 min. | **TOTAL TIME** 45 min. | **SERVES** 4

1. Heat the broiler and line a rimmed baking sheet with nonstick foil.

2. Tear the baguette into pieces and soak in ¼ cup water until absorbed, then squeeze out all the moisture and transfer to a large bowl. Add the eggs, chopped garlic, chopped spinach, Parmesan, oregano and ½ teaspoon each salt and pepper and mix to combine. Add the beef and mix until combined. Form into tiny balls (about 1 level teaspoon each, about 92 balls) and place on the prepared baking sheet. Broil until browned, 6 to 8 minutes.

3. Halve the tomatoes and arrange, cut sides up, on the second baking sheet. Drizzle with the oil and sprinkle with pressed garlic and a pinch each salt and pepper. Broil until the garlic is fragrant, 3 to 4 minutes. Serve the meatballs with the tomatoes and the sliced spinach.

PER SERVING *About 310 calories, 16.5 g fat (5.5 g saturated fat), 29 g protein, 505 mg sodium, 11 g carbohydrates, 2 g fiber*

TIP Cook the meatballs and refrigerate for up to 4 days. Warm in the microwave or oven along with the tomatoes.

Slow Roasted Lamb with Pistachio Gremolata

3 garlic cloves, finely chopped

2 teaspoons ground coriander

Kosher salt and pepper

1 boneless leg of lamb (about
4 pounds), trimmed of excess fat

1 pound thin carrots, quartered
lengthwise

1 pound parsnips, quartered
lengthwise

2 medium leeks, sliced

2 tablespoons olive oil

½ cup shelled salted
roasted pistachios

½ cup packed mint leaves

½ cup packed flat-leaf parsley leaves

2 teaspoons grated lemon zest

ACTIVE TIME 20 min. | **TOTAL TIME** 1 hr. 45 min. | **SERVES** 6

1. Heat the oven to 325°F. In a small bowl, combine the garlic, coriander, 2 teaspoons salt and 1 teaspoon pepper. Rub all over the lamb. Roll the lamb into a cylinder. With kitchen string, tie the lamb in 2-inch intervals to hold its shape. Place on a rack fitted into a foil-lined rimmed baking sheet. Roast for 1 hour.

2. Increase the oven temperature to 475°F. On another rimmed baking sheet, toss the carrots, parsnips and leeks with the oil and ¼ teaspoon salt. Roast the vegetables and lamb for 30 minutes or until the vegetables are tender and the lamb is cooked to your desired doneness (145°F for medium), stirring vegetables once.

3. Meanwhile, on a cutting board, combine the pistachios, mint, parsley and lemon zest; chop finely. Remove the string and slice the lamb. Serve with the vegetables, sprinkled with the gremolata.

PER SERVING *About 380 calories, 16 g fat (5 g saturated fat), 37 g protein, 715 mg sodium, 22 g carbohydrates, 6 g fiber*

4 uncooked breakfast sausages
(about 6 ounces total)

4 slices bacon

8 ounces small cremini mushrooms,
halved or quartered if large

16 Campari or cocktail
tomatoes, halved

2 garlic cloves, finely chopped

1 tablespoon olive oil

Kosher salt and pepper

4 large eggs

½ cup chopped fresh flat-leaf parsley

Toast, for serving (optional)

‹Sheet Pan Sausage & Egg Breakfast Bake

ACTIVE TIME 15 min. | **TOTAL TIME** 50 min. | **SERVES** 4

1. Heat the oven to 400°F. On a rimmed baking sheet, roast the sausages and bacon for 15 minutes.

2. In a large bowl, toss the mushrooms, tomatoes and garlic with the oil and a pinch each of salt and pepper. Add to baking sheet and roast 10 minutes.

3. Make wells among the vegetables and crack 1 egg into each space; return to the oven and roast until the sausage is cooked through and the egg whites are opaque throughout, 8 to 10 minutes more.

4. Sprinkle with the parsley and serve with toast if desired.

PER SERVING *About 300 calories, 21 g fat (6.5 g saturated fat), 17 g protein, 485 mg sodium, 10 g carbohydrates, 2 g fiber*

---

8 ounces tomatillos (about
10 small), husked

1 jalapeño, halved and seeded

1 tablespoon olive oil

Kosher salt

8 small corn tortillas

6 ounces sharp Cheddar cheese,
coarsely shredded (about 2 cups)

8 large eggs

2 cups cilantro leaves

2 tablespoons lime juice

Chopped cooked bacon and sliced
radishes, for serving (optional)

≡ QUICK & EASY ≡

Breakfast Tacos

ACTIVE TIME 10 min. | **TOTAL TIME** 20 min. | **SERVES** 4

1. Arrange one oven rack 6 inches from the broiler and another below that, about 12 inches from the broiler; heat broiler. On a rimmed baking sheet, toss the tomatillos and jalapeño with the oil and a pinch of salt. Broil on the top rack until tender and charred in spots, 8 to 10 minutes. Transfer to a blender.

2. Meanwhile, place the tortillas on a second rimmed baking sheet. Top each tortilla with ¼ cup Cheddar, leaving a slight well in the center. Top each with an egg (the cheese should prevent the eggs from spilling off the tortillas). Broil on the middle rack to your desired doneness, 4 to 6 minutes for a runny yolk.

3. Add the cilantro, lime juice and ¼ teaspoon salt to the vegetables in the blender and puree until smooth. Serve the salsa on the tacos with bacon and radishes if desired.

PER SERVING *About 435 calories, 28 g fat (13 g saturated fat), 25 g protein, 560 mg sodium, 22 g carbohydrates, 5 g fiber*

TIP Make this easy go-to breakfast vegetarian by simply omitting the bacon. Adding vegetable-based protein breakfast sausages is also an option.

2¼ cups all-purpose flour

2 teaspoons baking powder

½ teaspoon baking soda

1 teaspoon kosher salt

2¼ cups buttermilk

2 large eggs, at room temperature

¼ cup sugar

1 tablespoon honey

1 teaspoon pure vanilla extract

4 tablespoons unsalted butter

1 pint blueberries

1 cup maple syrup

Yogurt, for serving (optional)

Sheet Pan Pancakes with Blueberry Syrup

ACTIVE TIME 15 min. | **TOTAL TIME** 35 min. | **SERVES** 12

1. Place a rimmed baking sheet on the center rack of the oven. Heat the oven to 450°F.

2. In a large bowl, whisk together the flour, baking powder, baking soda and salt. In a second bowl, whisk together the buttermilk, eggs, sugar, honey and vanilla. Melt 3 tablespoons of the butter and whisk it into buttermilk mixture. Pour the wet ingredients over the dry ones and fold just until no traces of flour remain (batter will be lumpy).

3. Carefully remove the hot pan from the oven and swirl the remaining tablespoon butter all over bottom to melt. Immediately pour in the batter and quickly spread evenly.

4. Bake until golden brown and a toothpick inserted in the center comes out clean, 13 to 15 minutes.

5. Meanwhile, in a microwave-safe bowl, combine the blueberries and syrup and microwave on medium power until heated through, about 3 minutes. Serve over pancake with yogurt if desired.

PER SERVING *About 265 calories, 6 g fat (3.5 g saturated fat), 6 g protein, 370 mg sodium, 48 g carbohydrates, 1 g fiber*

TIP For a different flavor, swap blueberries for blackberries or sliced strawberries.

SWITCH IT UP!

Adjust the herbs and cheese to your tastes. We use thyme and Cheddar in this recipe, but you can mix and match herbs and cheeses to suit your preferences. (Basil and mozzarella would be one delicious combo, for example.)

Go vegetarian. If you're trying to feed a crowd with some dietary restrictions, have no fear: This recipe is just as tasty minus the ham and plus sautéed mushrooms, spinach, or broccoli.

Make it sweet instead of savory. Craving something a little sweeter? Stir some sugar and spices into the milk mixture, and replace the ham and cheese with berries.

Nonstick cooking spray

2 1/2 cups low-fat (1 percent) milk

8 large eggs

2 tablespoons Dijon mustard

1 teaspoon chopped fresh thyme

Kosher salt and pepper

1 large baguette, thinly sliced

8 ounces Cheddar cheese, shredded

8 ounces thinly sliced deli ham

1 tablespoon snipped fresh chives

‹ Ham & Cheese Overnight Casserole

ACTIVE TIME 20 min. | **TOTAL TIME** 2 hr. 20 min. | **SERVES** 6

1. Spray a square 2-quart baking dish with cooking spray.

2. In a bowl, whisk the milk, eggs, mustard, thyme and 1/4 teaspoon each salt and pepper to blend.

3. Arrange half of the bread, overlapping, in the baking dish. Pour half of the milk mixture over the bread; sprinkle with half of the Cheddar. Top with the ham, then repeat layering of bread, milk and Cheddar. Cover the dish and chill 1 hour or up to overnight.

4. Heat the oven to 350°F. Uncover and bake until golden and the custard is set, 50 to 55 minutes. Let stand 5 minutes before serving. Garnish with chives.

PER SERVING *About 481 calories, 22 g fat (10 g saturated fat), 33 g protein, 1,250 mg sodium, 36 g carbohydrates, 1 g fiber*

4 everything bagels, toasted and chopped

6 large eggs

2 cups milk

4 ounces Monterey Jack cheese, shredded

4 slices cooked bacon, finely chopped

4 scallions, sliced, plus more for topping

Kosher salt and pepper

Bagel Breakfast Bake

ACTIVE TIME 15 min. | **TOTAL TIME** 2 hr. 15 min. | **SERVES** 6

1. Arrange the bagels in a 2- to 2 1/2-quart baking dish.

2. In a large bowl, whisk together the eggs, milk, Monterey Jack, bacon, sliced scallions, 1/2 teaspoon salt and 1/4 teaspoon pepper. Pour the egg mixture over the bagels, pressing down slightly to submerge. Cover and refrigerate 1 hour or up to overnight.

3. Heat the oven to 350°F. Uncover the dish and bake for 45 to 55 minutes until set. Let cool 15 minutes before serving; sprinkle with scallions.

PER SERVING *About 434 calories, 16 g fat (7 g saturated fat), 23 g protein, 1,127 mg sodium, 48 g carbohydrates, 3 g fiber*

Oil for the dish

4 large eggs

1½ cups whole milk

1 tablespoon Dijon mustard

⅛ teaspoon ground nutmeg

Kosher salt and pepper

1 loaf French or Italian bread,
cut into 2-inch pieces

1 small red onion, cut into
¼-inch-thick wedges

1 crisp red apple (such as Gala or
Braeburn), cored and thinly sliced

4 ounces sliced ham, torn into
2-inch pieces

3 ounces sharp Cheddar
cheese, shredded

Green salad, for serving (optional)

‹ Ham, Cheddar &
Red Onion Bread Pudding

ACTIVE TIME 15 min. | **TOTAL TIME** 1 hr. 5 min. | **SERVES** 6

1. Heat the oven to 350°F. Oil a 2½- to 3-quart baking dish.

2. In a large bowl, whisk together the eggs, milk, mustard, nutmeg and
¼ teaspoon each salt and pepper. Add the bread and let sit, tossing
occasionally, for 5 minutes.

3. Fold the onion, apple, ham and Cheddar into the bread mixture. Transfer
to the prepared baking dish. Bake until set and a knife inserted in the center
comes out clean (cover the bread pudding with foil if it browns too quickly),
45 to 50 minutes. Serve with salad if desired.

PER SERVING *About 270 calories, 10.5 g fat (4.5 g saturated fat), 14 g protein,
650 mg sodium, 29 g carbohydrates, 2 g fiber*

4 tablespoons melted butter

24 soft slider rolls, split

8 ounces sharp Cheddar cheese,
thinly sliced

8 ounces dill pickle slices, drained and
patted dry

2 plum tomatoes, seeded and very
thinly sliced

8 ounces thinly sliced smoked ham

1 tablespoon dried onion flakes

2 teaspoons poppy seeds

⇒ FAMILY FRIENDLY ⇐

Ham & Cheese Oven Sliders

ACTIVE TIME 15 min. | **TOTAL TIME** 50 min. | **SERVES** 10

1. Heat the oven to 375°F. Brush the bottom of a 13-inch by 9-inch baking dish
with half of the melted butter. Line the dish with the bottoms of the rolls.

2. Onto the rolls in the dish, layer the Cheddar, pickle slices, tomatoes and then
ham. Replace the tops of the rolls. Cover the dish with foil; bake for 20 minutes.

3. Meanwhile, combine the dried onions and poppy seeds. Uncover the
baking dish. Brush the tops of the rolls with the remaining butter. Sprinkle
with the onion–poppy seed mixture. Bake 10 to 15 minutes or until deep
golden brown on top.

PER SERVING *About 300 calories, 15 g fat (8 g saturated fat), 12 g protein,
600 mg sodium, 29 g carbohydrates, 1 g fiber*

Chapter 4

The Skillet

For quick and easy one-pot meals, a 12-inch skillet stands out. It's the pan to grab for sautéing everything from onions and aromatics to vegetables or meat, and it simmers sauces like a dream. It can even go into the oven for the final minutes of cooking time to finish dishes with crusty-top perfection. We recommend keeping an assortment of different-sized skillets made of different materials on hand to tackle a wide range of cooking tasks.

Which material is best?

When choosing what type of cookware is right for you, you'll first have to decide between cast iron, ceramic cookware, nonstick cookware or traditional stainless steel. We'll walk you through the range of skillet options, providing the pros and cons of each material, below.

Cast iron This skillet is one of the most versatile pans you can buy and popular among chefs because it heats and cooks evenly, can reach high temperatures and holds temperature well. It can be used for almost everything, from getting a good sear on meat to making a frittata and popping it in the oven.

Ceramic Cookware glazed with a ceramic coating offers a good alternative to traditional nonstick pans. Some are made from clay, baked in a kiln and glazed, but the majority are metal glazed with ceramic. The downside to ceramic cookware is its glaze tends to wear quicker than traditional nonstick, and it isn't as durable as good stainless cookware that could last forever.

Nonstick At least one nonstick pan is essential in every cook's kitchen. There are two main types of nonstick cookware: traditional nonstick and ceramic. The difference lies in the nonstick coating and sometimes the material of the pan.

Stainless steel These pans can handle screaming-hot temperatures. Most stainless steel cookware has a core or interior made from aluminum for even heating. Stainless steel cookware also lacks a nonstick coating, which some prefer. That said, contrary to the name, stainless steel pans are prone to staining since food sticks to the surface more than other materials. Stock up on a great stainless steel cleaner (we prefer Bar Keepers Friend) if you want to keep them clean and fresh.

How to Choose a Skillet

What size skillet do I need?
Skillets are measured in diameter. Here's a breakdown of the sizes that get the most use and what they are typically best for.

8 inches and under Smaller pans are good for single-serve meals. Make an omelet in a small nonstick, or pop a mini cast iron skillet right into the toaster oven without having to power up your entire stove or oven.

10 inches This is a popular size. Ten-inch pans can handle one to two steaks at a time, or up to four chicken thighs, ideal for a family of four. They're also a medium weight, so you won't struggle when moving them from the range to the oven.

11 inches and above Bigger pans are good for a family or for batch cooking. The tradeoff is that they can get quite heavy, so make sure you're able to lift it.

Are there other features to consider?
These design considerations can make all the difference in your cooking experience. Consider the following "extras" when shopping for new skillets.

Helper handles This small handle opposite the main handle makes lifting and storing pans easier. You'll especially want to prioritize these on larger or heavier pans.

Pour spouts It's ideal to have one pour spout on each side. These lips make pouring grease out during cooking easier, which promotes browned, crispy, seared food. Spouts are also useful for making a sauce right in the pan and easily pouring it over your food.

Edges Look for rounded edges that slope outward slightly instead of straight edges you might find on a saucepan. This shape allows for more airflow, which makes for a crispier finish and better sear.

SAUSAGE & CHEESE
SKILLET LASAGNA 107

Nonstick and Ceramic Skillet Care

::::::::::::::::::::::::::

Follow these general guidelines to prolong the life of nonstick skillets.

Never heat an empty pan. Nonstick pans will get hotter much faster and approach the 500°F mark quicker.

Use medium or low heat. Refer to the manufacturer's instructions for what temperature is best, but nonstick pans will heat nicely on lower settings.

Use less oil. Unlike cooking in a stainless steel skillet, you won't need as much oil to prevent foods from sticking.

Avoid using metal utensils. These tools can scratch the nonstick coating even if your instruction says you can use them.

Avoid putting nonstick cookware in the dishwasher. The dishwasher wears down the coating faster than handwashing.

IS NONSTICK COOKWARE SAFE?

Traditional nonstick pans have gotten a bad rap because many are made with Teflon (also known as PTFE) which, at high temperatures releases compounds into the air that are linked to some cancers. Today, many nonstick pans are made without PTFE, but, either way, nonstick cookware is safe if you use it with the right temperatures. How hot is too hot? PTFE starts to decompose at 500°F and more significantly at 660°F, so use your nonstick pans on medium or low heat.

Stainless Steel Skillet Care

::::::::::::::::::::::::::

Follow these general guidelines to keep your stainless steel pan sparkling.

Heat the pan before adding oil. Unlike nonstick skillets, this will help prevent food from sticking to the surface. The steel becomes static, which creates a temporary nonstick surface.

Use more oil. Evenly coating the pan with oil or another grease can help prevent sticky spots. If the oil is shimmering, swirl it around the pan and you're good to go.

Avoid overheating the pan. Steel is very effective at holding heat, so if you heat the pan on high it might lead to screaming temperatures and burned food.

Let meat come to room temperature. Cold food is more likely to stick when it contracts in a hot steel pan. Allow meat, chicken and fish to sit for 10 to 15 minutes before cooking.

Cool the pan before washing it. Soaking a hot pan in cold water could cause warping.

Use some elbow grease. Cleaning stainless steel takes some effort, especially if food has burned on. Use a stainless steel cleaner like Bar Keepers Friend with a non-abrasive cleaning pad. Still calling SOS? Fill the pot with hot water and a generous squirt or two of dishwashing liquid. Put it back on the stove to simmer for 15 to 30 minutes, carefully loosening the burned bits with a spatula as they soften. When done, empty the pot and scrub clean.

TOP-TESTED CAST IRON SKILLET

While we haven't conducted a cross-category test of cast iron pans, our pros have road tested them in the Lab and in home kitchens where they get an even more extensive workout. Our favorites include traditional cast iron skillets, as well as ones that are preseasoned and others that are enameled and easier to clean.

BEST OVERALL
Lodge 12-inch Cast Iron Skillet
In addition to being a great value, Lodge cast iron pans are made to last. This 12-inch cast iron skillet arrives preseasoned so you can start cooking right away, and the pan heats evenly, making it one of our favorites for cooking larger batches of food without fear of the center overheating or the edges being too cool. We also like the short handle, in addition to its relatively light weight (4¼ pounds), which makes moving it on and off the burner easy. This pick comes with a red silicone handle protector to help keep the handle cool, or you can pick from a couple of colors and materials.

TOP-TESTED CERAMIC SKILLET

We tested ceramic skillets to see how well they distribute heat, if they can evenly sear a steak, how quickly they can bring water to a boil and how well they are able to simmer sauce without burning it. We also evaluated their handles for ease of use and accessed how much effort was needed to clean them. For ceramic pans, we test their nonstick-ability by cooking eggs and pancakes with no grease.

BEST OVERALL
**GreenPan Revolution
Ceramic Nonstick Skillet**
This ceramic skillet, made of anodized aluminum with stainless steel handles and a ceramic nonstick finish, was a top scorer in our multiple tests. It heated very evenly whether we used gas, electric or induction. Omelets slid right out of the pan, steaks seared perfectly, and pancakes browned evenly without the need for extra butter. It also aced our scorch test, which means, no need to stir soups or stews while they simmer. If you're looking to crisp up the topping on a casserole, note that you can put GreenPan Revolution's pans in the oven, up to 600°F. Cleanup is easy, too, because unlike many nonstick pans, you can pop these ceramic pieces in the dishwasher.

**SCAN FOR
MORE SKILLET
LAB REVIEWS**

TOP-TESTED NONSTICK SKILLET

We've tested more than 80 nonstick cookware sets. We put 15 additional nonstick pans to the test this year alone to find the best ones, using more than 120 eggs and 15 steaks, to evaluate how well each released food without sticking or leaving behind residue, how they handled, including weight and balance and how easy they were to clean. We looked for ones that were durable, could withstand high temperatures and, most importantly, were very nonstick.

BEST OVERALL
Le Creuset Toughened
Nonstick Pro 12-inch Fry Pan

This pan has a thick, solid handle and is heavier than most nonstick pans of the past that were thin and flimsy. In our tests, eggs only needed a shake to release from the pan and scrambled eggs cleaned up with just a touch of the sponge. It can handle tougher feats as well; it seared steak evenly on both sides and is oven-safe up to 500°F.

Made of anodized aluminum, which gives it some heft, and a nonstick finish that's Teflon-free, this pan combines unbeatable performance with durability. It's dishwasher-safe, and we love that the handles stay cool while cooking. We were blown away by the outstanding heat distribution, quick boiling and even searing. The nonstick coating was so effective that we could scramble eggs or sauté vegetables without oil or butter.

TOP-TESTED STAINLESS STEEL SKILLET

We evaluated more than 100 cookware sets over the years. We tested how evenly skillets distributed heat on gas and electric ranges, how well they browned meat and how well they maintained a steady simmer and resisted scorching sauce. Our favorite nonstick pans are the ones that can do it all, from cooking an egg with no oil to searing a steak, while remaining easy to clean after use.

BEST OVERALL
Hestan NanoBond Stainless Steel Skillet

This pan excelled in our tests. It's made of ultra-strong titanium bonded to stainless steel, which makes it super durable; plus, it's oven- and broiler-safe up to 500°F so you can use it for practically anything. Steak seared beautifully and evenly, while water came to a boil quickly in the saucepan and sauce maintained a steady simmer and later washed right off.

After testing and using the frying pan consistently, we can confidently say that barely anything sticks to these pans (even though they're not nonstick!) and they're the easiest stainless steel pans to clean. Stubborn bits just required a soak versus a ton of elbow grease like others we tested. Their silver color deepens over time but can look like new again with their special cleaner.

Cast Iron Care

::::::::::::::::::::::::::::::

One of the best things about cast iron is its ability to get better with time. When cared for properly, the seasoning (the cast iron code for "nonstick") improves and you don't need to add any cooking oils to the pan. When a pan comes preseasoned, it means that the company has already created a nonstick coating for you by coating the pan with a thin layer of oil and allowing it to heat long enough to absorb the oil into the pores of the metal. It's up to you to continue building on the seasoning as you use your skillet. Cast iron skillets can last a lifetime if cared for properly—one brand we feature even offers a 100-year warranty.

While some people believe maintaining and cleaning cast iron is difficult, it's actually quite simple. Some use soap while others use strictly water, but either way the key is to thoroughly dry the skillet before putting it away.

How to Clean a Cast Iron Pan

Never allow cast iron to soak in water or put it in the dishwasher. Here's the best way to care for your pan.

1. After cooking, let the pan cool completely, then pour out any drippings. Use a nylon or wooden scraper and running water to remove food particles.

2. Wash the pan with a stiff bristled brush (not a scouring pad) and mild dish soap if needed, then wipe dry.

3. Set the pan on a hot burner for 30 seconds or until the remaining moisture evaporates. A bone-dry skillet is less likely to rust.

4. Turn off the heat and use a paper towel to carefully rub a few drops of vegetable oil onto the inner surface. After the pan cools fully, store it with a fresh paper towel on its surface to absorb any lingering wetness.

How to Season a New Cast Iron Pan

Cast iron pans that have not been preseasoned by the manufacturer require some care before you use them. Seasoning the cookware creates a clean surface to cook food evenly, stops your food from sticking, and helps prevent rust.

1. Wash your new pan with hot, soapy water. Dry it thoroughly.

2. Using a cloth saturated with vegetable oil, rub the entire surface of the pan, including the exterior.

3. Heat the pan upside down in a 350°F oven for 1 hour. Turn off the oven and let the pan cool completely before storing.

HOW TO CLEAN WITHOUT SOAP

To clean cast iron without soap and water: After cooking, coat the bottom of the pan with kosher salt and use a wooden scraper to scrape up food bits. Once it's cool, toss out the salt and wipe the pan with a dry paper towel.

Cooking Tips for Best Results

Here are a few tips to help you pick out the best new skillet and use it wisely.

1. For browning, your best bet is a pan with low sides and a large surface area. It can hold more pieces at once, and foods won't steam as they brown.

2. If you're making a skillet dinner, opt for a deep pan that can hold lots of vegetables and sauce.

3. When it comes to searing steaks, choose cast iron or stainless over nonstick pans.

4. For long simmers, cast iron's a good choice. And in fact, if you need more iron in your diet, regularly cooking in cast iron can up your levels.

5. If you'll be using your skillet in the oven to brown a frittata or finish cooking fish, stick with cast iron and stainless steel, watch out for plastic handles and check the oven-temperature limitations before you buy.

6. The secret to turning out great omelets is to use a nonstick skillet with sloped sides.

7. Don't use nonstick cooking sprays from an aerosol can on nonstick surfaces. They won't help and will result in a gunky buildup that detracts from rather than enhances the finish. Use oil or another type of grease instead.

8. To keep stainless steel looking new, equip yourself with a good scrubbing pad and the cleaner called Bar Keepers Friend.

TUNISIAN SKILLET CHICKEN 123

2 cups packed torn crustless stale white bread

½ cup crumbled feta cheese

⅓ cup finely chopped fresh mint, plus more for topping

3 garlic cloves, pressed

Kosher salt and pepper

2 pounds ground lamb or beef chuck (80 percent lean)

1 tablespoon extra virgin olive oil

1 medium onion, finely chopped

1 28-ounce can crushed tomatoes

1 cup low-sodium beef or chicken broth

2 tablespoons oregano leaves

2 bay leaves

1½ cups shredded mozzarella cheese

◄ Doubly Cheesy Meatball Bake

ACTIVE TIME 15 min. | **TOTAL TIME** 1 hr. 45 min. | **SERVES** 6

1. Heat the oven to 375°F. In a large bowl, soak the bread in cold water for 20 minutes. Squeeze out and discard the excess water from the bread.

2. To the bowl with the soaked bread, add the feta, mint, garlic and ½ teaspoon each salt and pepper, tossing to combine. Add the lamb and mix until just combined; form into twelve 2-inch meatballs.

3. In a 12-inch cast iron skillet, heat the oil on medium-high. Add the meatballs; cook for 10 minutes, turning, until browned on two sides. Transfer to a large plate. Pour off the excess fat from the pan, leaving a thin coating. Scrape up any browned bits and reduce the heat to medium. Add the onion to the skillet and cook for 5 minutes, stirring. Add the tomatoes, broth, oregano, bay leaves and ¼ teaspoon salt, stirring to combine. Bring to a boil on high. Reduce the heat to simmer; cook for 15 minutes or until reduced slightly, stirring often. Add the meatballs to the tomato sauce; top with the mozzarella. Transfer the skillet to the oven and bake for 20 minutes.

4. Reset the oven to broil on high; broil 3 minutes or until the cheese has browned. Sprinkle with mint.

PER SERVING About 495 calories, 27 g fat (12 g saturated fat), 42 g protein, 1,015 mg sodium, 25 g carbohydrates, 4 g fiber

¼ cup all-purpose flour

2 tablespoons olive oil

1 small onion, chopped

1 stalk celery, chopped

½ small green bell pepper, chopped

½ teaspoon dried basil

¼ teaspoon cayenne

¼ teaspoon dried thyme

Kosher salt and coarsely ground black pepper

1 8-ounce bottle clam juice

1 12-ounce bag large shrimp, shelled and deveined

Cooked white rice, for serving

2 scallions, chopped, for topping

Shrimp Etouffee

ACTIVE TIME 15 min. | **TOTAL TIME** 40 min. | **SERVES** 4

1. Meanwhile, in a nonstick 10-inch skillet, cook the flour on medium-high, stirring and shaking the pan frequently, until the flour turns a nutty brown, 6 to 8 minutes. Transfer the flour to a small bowl; set aside. Wipe the skillet clean.

2. In same skillet, heat the olive oil on medium until hot. Add the onion, celery, green pepper, basil, cayenne, thyme, ½ teaspoon salt and ¼ teaspoon pepper, and cook until the vegetables are tender, about 10 minutes, stirring often.

3. Increase the heat to medium-high. Sprinkle the cooked flour over the vegetable mixture; stir until blended. Gradually stir in the clam juice and ¾ cup water, whisking constantly until the mixture boils; boil 1 minute. Add the shrimp and cook 3 to 4 minutes longer or until the shrimp turn opaque throughout. Serve the shrimp mixture over the rice; sprinkle with scallions.

PER SERVING About 349 calories, 8 g fat (1 g saturated fat), 17 g protein, 862 mg sodium, 50 g carbohydrates, 2 g fiber

1/3 cup reduced-sodium soy sauce, divided

2 tablespoons lime juice

2 tablespoons packed brown sugar

1 tablespoon grated peeled fresh ginger

2 garlic cloves, grated

1 to 2 teaspoons sriracha

1 teaspoon sesame oil

3 teaspoons cornstarch, divided

1 pound sirloin or strip steak, halved lengthwise and thinly sliced

1 large head broccoli (about 1 pound), cut into small florets, stem peeled (if necessary) and sliced

1 tablespoon canola oil

Cooked white rice, for serving

Chopped scallions and sesame seeds, for serving (optional)

Beef & Broccoli

ACTIVE TIME 30 min. | **TOTAL TIME** 30 min. | **SERVES** 4

1. In a medium bowl, whisk together the soy sauce, lime juice, brown sugar, ginger, garlic, sriracha, sesame oil and 2 teaspoons of the cornstarch. Transfer half (about 1/3 cup) to a small bowl and whisk in the remaining teaspoon cornstarch and 1/3 cup water; set aside.

2. Add the steak to the remaining sauce, toss to coat and let marinate for 15 minutes.

3. Meanwhile, heat a large skillet on medium. Add 1/2 cup water and bring to a simmer. Add the broccoli and cook, covered, until bright green and just barely tender, 4 to 5 minutes. Transfer the broccoli to a plate.

4. Wipe out the skillet. Heat the canola oil on medium-high. Remove the steak from the marinade and cook it in a single layer in batches until browned, 2 minutes per side. Return the first batch of steak to the skillet, add the sauce, and simmer until it is beginning to thicken, 2 to 3 minutes. Add the broccoli and toss to combine.

5. Serve over rice, sprinkled with scallions and sesame seeds if desired.

PER SERVING *About 370 calories, 19.5 g fat, (6.5 g saturated fat), 29 g protein, 905 mg sodium, 21 g carbohydrates, 4 g fiber*

TIP **Keep this recipe quick and easy by using precooked rice.**

HOW TO CUT MEAT AGAINST THE GRAIN

For the most delicious pieces, thinly slice the beef against the grain before cooking. To identify the direction of the grain, look for parallel lines in the muscle fiber running through the meat. You will want to cut perpendicular to them. This will shorten the muscle fibers and make the beef more tender when cooked.

‹ Pork Chops with Rosemary-Truffle Sauce

2 tablespoons extra virgin olive oil

4 bone-in pork chops (each about 1 inch thick)

Kosher salt and pepper

3 medium shallots, chopped

12 ounces cremini mushrooms, thinly sliced

½ teaspoon chopped fresh rosemary

⅔ cup half-and-half

2 tablespoons truffle butter

ACTIVE TIME 15 min. | **TOTAL TIME** 30 min. | **SERVES** 4

1. In a 12-inch skillet, heat the oil on medium-high until hot but not smoking. Season the pork chops all over with ½ teaspoon each salt and pepper. Cook the pork chops for 6 minutes or until browned on both sides, turning over once; transfer to a large plate. Reduce the heat to medium and pour off the excess fat in the skillet. To the skillet, add the shallots, mushrooms, rosemary and ⅛ teaspoon salt. Cook for 5 minutes, stirring.

2. Stir in the half-and-half and truffle butter. Nestle the pork chops in the sauce. Simmer for 4 to 6 minutes or until the pork is cooked through (145°F).

PER SERVING *About 400 calories, 25 g fat (10 g saturated fat), 33 g protein, 400 mg sodium, 9 g carbohydrates, 1 g fiber*

Sausage & Cheese Skillet Lasagna

1 tablespoon olive oil

1 pound sweet Italian sausage, casings removed

2 garlic cloves, chopped

2 cups chicken stock

2 cups marinara sauce

1 14½-ounce can diced tomatoes, drained

8 ounces lasagna noodles, broken into large pieces

⅔ cup roughly chopped fresh basil, plus more for topping

⅓ cup ricotta cheese

4 ounces mozzarella cheese, coarsely shredded (about 1 cup)

2 tablespoons grated Parmesan cheese

ACTIVE TIME 20 min. | **TOTAL TIME** 40 min. | **SERVES** 6

1. Heat the broiler. Heat the oil in a 12-inch cast iron skillet on medium. Add sausage and cook, breaking it up with a spoon, until beginning to brown, 4 to 6 minutes. Add garlic and cook, stirring, until fragrant, 1 minute.

2. Add chicken stock, marinara and tomatoes. Nestle pasta pieces in broth mixture, and bring to a boil. Reduce heat and simmer, covered, 4 minutes. Uncover and continue simmering, stirring occasionally, until pasta is tender, 10 to 12 minutes.

3. Remove from the heat and fold in the basil. Top with the ricotta, mozzarella and Parmesan. Broil until golden brown, 2 to 3 minutes.

PER SERVING *About 575 calories, 35 g fat (13 g saturated fat), 24 g protein, 1,338 mg sodium, 40 g carbohydrates, 4 g fiber*

1 tablespoon olive oil

5 ounces baby spinach, coarsely chopped

3 garlic cloves, chopped

1/2 cup ricotta cheese

1 1/2 ounces Parmesan cheese, grated (about 1/3 cup)

1 tablespoon lemon juice

1/4 teaspoon red pepper flakes

Kosher salt and ground black pepper

1 1/2 tablespoons cornmeal

Flour, for sprinkling

1 pound pizza dough, at room temperature

6 ounces Fontina cheese, shredded (about 1 1/2 cups)

1 14-ounce can artichoke hearts, drained and quartered

Torn basil leaves, for topping

Spinach-Artichoke Deep-Dish Pizza

ACTIVE TIME 15 min. | **TOTAL TIME** 40 min. | **SERVES** 4

1. Arrange an oven rack in the lowest position and heat the oven to 450°F. Heat the oil in an oven-safe 10-inch skillet on medium. Add the spinach and garlic and cook until the spinach is wilted and the liquid has evaporated, 3 to 4 minutes; transfer to a plate. Let the skillet cool slightly and wipe clean.

2. In a bowl, mix together the ricotta, Parmesan, lemon juice and red pepper flakes; season with salt and black pepper.

3. Sprinkle the skillet with the cornmeal. On a floured surface, stretch and shape the dough into a 12-inch round. Press into the bottom and up the sides of the skillet.

4. Top the dough with the ricotta mixture, spinach, Fontina and artichoke hearts. Bake until the crust is golden brown, 20 to 24 minutes.

5. Let sit for 5 minutes, then sprinkle with the basil and cut into wedges.

PER SERVING *About 405 calories, 18 g fat (8.5 g saturated fat), 18 g protein, 1,125 mg sodium, 40 g carbohydrates, 2 g fiber*

TIP **Make this recipe your own by adding favorite toppings. Try sliced cherry tomatoes, Kalamata olives and slivered red onions. Or thinly sliced pears, proscuitto and gorgonzola.**

‹ Seared Salmon with Charred Green Beans

2 tablespoons plus 2 teaspoons olive oil, divided

1¼ pounds skinless salmon fillet, cut into 4 portions

Kosher salt and pepper

1 pound green beans, trimmed

4 garlic cloves, smashed and thinly sliced

1 small red chile, thinly sliced

2 tablespoons capers, drained and patted dry

Lemon wedges, for serving (optional)

ACTIVE TIME 15 min. | **TOTAL TIME** 15 min. | **SERVES** 4

1. Heat 2 teaspoons of the oil in a large skillet on medium-high. Season the salmon with ½ teaspoon each salt and pepper, add to the skillet, flesh side down, reduce the heat to medium and cook until golden brown and just opaque throughout, 5 to 6 minutes per side. Remove from the heat and set aside.

2. Heat the remaining 2 tablespoons oil in a large cast-iron skillet on medium-high. Add the green beans and cook until browned on one side, 2½ minutes. Turn with tongs and cook until browned all over and just barely tender, about 3 minutes more.

3. Remove the pan from the heat and toss the green beans with ¼ teaspoon salt, then the garlic, chile and capers. Return to medium heat and cook, tossing, until the garlic is golden brown, 1 to 2 minutes. Serve with the salmon and lemon wedges if desired.

PER SERVING *About 285 calories, 14.5 g fat (2.5 g saturated fat), 31 g protein, 540 mg sodium, 9 g carbohydrates, 3 g fiber*

Spicy Shakshuka

2 tablespoons olive oil

1 onion, chopped

1 red bell pepper, cut into ¼-inch pieces

1 small red chile, finely chopped

Kosher salt and pepper

2 garlic cloves, finely chopped

1 teaspoon ground cumin

1 14½-ounce can whole tomatoes

4 large eggs

Snipped fresh chives, for topping (optional)

ACTIVE TIME 15 min. | **TOTAL TIME** 35 min. | **SERVES** 4

1. Heat the oil in a large skillet on medium. Add the onions and cook, covered, for 4 minutes. Add the bell pepper and chile, season with ½ teaspoon each salt and pepper, and cook, covered, until just tender, 6 to 8 minutes, stirring occasionally. Stir in the garlic and cumin; cook for 1 minute.

2. Crush the tomatoes with your hands and add to skillet along with their juices. Bring to a boil.

3. Reduce the heat and make 4 small wells in sauce; carefully crack 1 egg into each. Gently simmer, covered, for 6 minutes.

4. Uncover and cook until the whites are set and the yolks are cooked to desired doneness, 5 to 7 minutes for slightly runny yolks. Sprinkle with chives if desired.

PER SERVING *About 180 calories, 11.5 g fat (2.5 g saturated fat), 8 g protein, 465 mg sodium, 10 g carbohydrates, 2 g fiber*

1 large egg

1 pound skinless salmon fillet, finely chopped

2 scallions, chopped

3 tablespoons chopped fresh dill, divided

3 tablespoons chopped fresh flat-leaf parsley, divided

Kosher salt and pepper

1 tablespoon olive oil

½ cup Greek yogurt

1 teaspoon lemon zest

2 tablespoons lemon juice

4 brioche buns, toasted

8 Bibb lettuce leaves

2 Persian cucumbers or ½ English cucumber, shaved lengthwise

2 cups broccoli or radish sprouts

◂ Salmon Burgers

ACTIVE TIME 25 min. | **TOTAL TIME** 30 min. | **SERVES** 4

1. In a medium bowl, beat the egg until frothy. Fold in the salmon, scallions, 2 tablespoons each dill and parsley and ¼ teaspoon each salt and pepper.

2. Heat the oil in a large skillet on medium. Spoon four mounds of salmon mixture (about ½ cup each) into the skillet and flatten into ½-inch-thick patties. Cook the patties until golden brown, 2 minutes per side.

3. Meanwhile, in a bowl, combine the yogurt, lemon zest, lemon juice, remaining tablespoon each dill and parsley and ¼ teaspoon each salt and pepper.

4. Spread the yogurt sauce on bottom buns (about 2½ tablespoons each) and top with the lettuce, salmon patties, cucumber and sprouts; add top buns.

PER SERVING *About 398 calories, 14 g fat (4 g saturated fat), 34 g protein, 592 mg sodium, 33 g carbohydrates, 3 g fiber*

---

4 6-ounce skinless salmon fillets

Kosher salt and pepper

3 tablespoons all-purpose flour

2 tablespoons olive oil

3 garlic cloves, minced

¼ cup dry white wine, such as sauvignon blanc

¼ cup lemon juice (from about 2 lemons), plus lemon slices for serving

2 tablespoons rinsed and drained capers

2 tablespoons chopped fresh flat-leaf parsley

2 teaspoons unsalted butter

Lemony Salmon Piccata

ACTIVE TIME 15 min. | **TOTAL TIME** 25 min. | **SERVES** 4

1. Season the salmon with ½ teaspoon each salt and pepper. Add the flour to a shallow bowl and dredge the salmon, shaking off excess.

2. Heat the oil in a large cast iron or nonstick skillet on medium-high. Cook the salmon, turning once, until golden, about 2 minutes. Reduce the heat to medium and add the garlic; continue to cook for 1 minute. Add the wine, lemon juice, capers and parsley; simmer on medium-low until the salmon is just cooked through, 5 to 6 minutes. Remove the pan from the heat. Add the butter; stir until melted, about 30 seconds.

3. Serve with lemon slices; top with the sauce before serving.

PER SERVING *About 413 calories, 26 g fat (6 g saturated fat), 39 g protein, 483 mg sodium, 7 g carbohydrates, 0 g fiber*

◄ Lemon Chicken & Pea Gemelli

ACTIVE TIME 20 min. | **TOTAL TIME** 20 min. | **SERVES** 4

2 tablespoons extra virgin olive oil

12 ounces boneless, skinless chicken breasts, cut into 2-inch pieces

Kosher salt and pepper

¼ cup lemon juice

4 cups low-sodium chicken broth

12 ounces gemelli or other short pasta

4 ounces cream cheese, at room temperature

1 cup peas, thawed if frozen

½ cup finely grated Parmesan cheese

2 teaspoons grated lemon zest

1 tablespoon finely chopped fresh tarragon

1. Heat the oil in a large, deep skillet on medium-high. Season the chicken with ¼ teaspoon each salt and pepper and cook until golden brown on all sides, 4 to 5 minutes; transfer to a large bowl. Add the lemon juice to the pan, scraping up the brown bits, then pour over the chicken in the bowl.

2. Add the broth and pasta to the skillet and bring to a boil. Reduce the heat and simmer, stirring often, for 10 minutes.

3. Return the chicken (and any juices) to the skillet and continue to cook until the pasta is just tender, about 3 minutes more.

4. Add the cream cheese, stirring to melt, then fold in the peas, Parmesan, lemon zest and tarragon.

PER SERVING *About 676 calories, 23.5 g fat (9 g saturated fat), 41 g protein, 535 mg sodium, 75 g carbohydrates, 5 g fiber*

Skillet-Roasted Chicken

ACTIVE TIME 15 min. | **TOTAL TIME** 1 hr. 30 min. | **SERVES** 4

2 small red onions, cut into ½-inch-thick wedges

1 small acorn squash (about 1¼ pounds), seeded and cut into 1½-inch-thick wedges

1 small fennel bulb, cut into ½-inch-thick wedges

1 tablespoon olive oil

12 thyme sprigs, divided, plus more for serving

Kosher salt and pepper

1 3½-pound chicken, giblets removed

2 rosemary sprigs

1. Heat the oven to 425°F. In a large cast iron skillet, toss the onions, squash and fennel with the oil, 4 thyme sprigs and ½ teaspoon each salt and pepper.

2. Season the chicken inside and out with 1½ teaspoons salt and ½ teaspoon pepper. Fold the wingtips back and underneath the chicken.

3. Place the chicken on top of the vegetables, breast side up; stuff the rosemary and the remaining thyme inside the cavity and loosely tie the legs together with kitchen string. Roast for 40 minutes.

4. Spoon and baste any pan juices over the chicken and continue roasting until it is golden brown and an instant-read thermometer inserted in the thickest part of the thigh registers 155°F to 165°F, 15 to 20 minutes more.

5. Transfer the vegetables to a platter, then carefully tilt the chicken to empty any juices from the cavity. Discard the herb sprigs. Transfer the chicken to a cutting board and let rest for at least 10 minutes before carving. Skim the fat from the juices in the skillet to serve over the chicken if desired. Serve the chicken with the vegetables.

PER SERVING *About 520 calories, 27.5 g fat (7 g saturated fat), 50 g protein, 1,130 mg sodium, 18 g carbohydrates, 4 g fiber*

3 tablespoons olive oil, divided

1½ pounds boneless, skinless chicken breasts, cut into 2½-inch pieces

Kosher salt and pepper

1 large onion, chopped

1 large red bell pepper, cut into ¼-inch pieces

4 garlic cloves, finely chopped

3 tablespoons all-purpose flour

1½ tablespoons paprika (Hungarian if possible)

1 cup low-sodium chicken broth

1 14-ounce can whole tomatoes, drained and chopped

½ to 1 teaspoon hot sauce (optional)

½ cup sour cream

Cooked egg noodles, for serving

Chopped fresh flat-leaf parsley, for topping

‹ Chicken Paprikash

ACTIVE TIME 35 min. | **TOTAL TIME** 35 min. | **SERVES** 4

1. Heat 2 tablespoons of the oil in a large skillet on medium-high. Season the chicken with ¼ teaspoon each salt and pepper and cook until golden brown, 2 to 3 minutes per side; transfer to a plate.

2. Reduce the heat to medium, add the remaining tablespoon oil to the skillet along with the onion and cook, stirring occasionally, for 5 minutes. Add the bell pepper and garlic and cook, stirring, for 2 minutes.

3. Sprinkle the vegetables with the flour and cook, stirring, for 2 minutes. Sprinkle with the paprika and cook, stirring, for 1 minute. Stir in the chicken broth, then the tomatoes; simmer for 5 minutes.

4. Return the chicken to the skillet along with any juices and the hot sauce (if using) and simmer until the chicken is cooked through, 5 to 8 minutes.

5. Remove from the heat and stir in the sour cream. Serve over egg noodles and sprinkle with parsley.

PER SERVING *About 425 calories, 20.5 g fat (5 g saturated fat), 43 g protein, 305 mg sodium, 17 g carbohydrates, 4 g fiber*

1 tablespoon olive oil

1 large onion, finely chopped

Kosher salt and pepper

1½ tablespoons grated peeled fresh ginger

2 garlic cloves, finely chopped

1 tablespoon curry powder

1 cup long-grain white rice

1 pound medium shrimp, peeled and deveined

1 cup frozen peas, thawed

1 cup chopped fresh cilantro

Lemon wedges, for serving (optional)

Indian Spiced Rice with Shrimp & Peas

ACTIVE TIME 20 min. | **TOTAL TIME** 30 min. | **SERVES** 4

1. Heat the oil in a large skillet on medium. Add the onion, season with ¼ teaspoon each salt and pepper, and cook, covered, stirring occasionally, until tender, 6 to 8 minutes. Add the ginger and garlic and cook, stirring, for 2 minutes. Add the curry powder and cook, stirring, for 1 minute.

2. Add the rice and stir to coat in the onion mixture. Stir in 2 cups water and bring to a boil. Reduce the heat and simmer, covered, for 15 minutes.

3. Fold the shrimp and peas into the partially cooked rice and cook, covered, until the shrimp are opaque throughout and the rice is tender, 4 to 5 minutes more.

4. Remove from the heat and fold in the cilantro. Serve with lemon wedges if desired.

PER SERVING *About 345 calories, 5.5 g fat (1 g saturated fat), 22 g protein, 790 mg sodium, 51 g carbohydrates, 4 g fiber*

Chicken Scarpariello

2 tablespoons olive oil

8 ounces sweet Italian sausage, casings removed, cut into 1½-inch pieces

6 small chicken thighs

Kosher salt and pepper

1 large onion, chopped

1 small red bell pepper, cut into ¼-inch pieces

8 garlic cloves, sliced

¾ cup dry white wine

¾ cup low-sodium chicken broth

½ cup chopped Peppadew peppers, plus ⅓ cup brine

1 teaspoon chopped fresh rosemary

Chopped fresh flat-leaf parsley, for topping

Crusty bread, for serving (optional)

ACTIVE TIME 30 min. | **TOTAL TIME** 55 min. | **SERVES** 4

1. Heat the oven to 450°F. Heat the oil in large oven-safe skillet on medium-high. Add the sausage to the pan and cook, turning twice, until browned, 5 to 6 minutes; transfer to a plate (sausage will not be fully cooked).

2. Reduce the heat to medium. Season the chicken with ¼ teaspoon each salt and pepper and cook until golden brown, 6 to 8 minutes; transfer to the plate.

3. Discard all but 2 tablespoons fat from the pan, then add the onion and bell pepper and sauté for 5 minutes. Stir in the garlic and sauté for 2 minutes. Stir in the wine and simmer for 4 minutes. Add the chicken broth, Peppadew peppers and brine and rosemary and bring to a simmer.

4. Nestle the chicken in the vegetables, transfer the skillet to the oven, and roast for 8 minutes. Nestle the sausage in the vegetables and continue roasting until the chicken is cooked through, about 6 minutes more. Sprinkle with parsley and serve with bread if desired.

PER SERVING *About 635 calories, 42 g fat, (12.5 g saturated fat), 48 g protein, 885 mg sodium, 13 g carbohydrates, 2 g fiber*

Mushroom & Bacon Dutch Baby

1 pound mixed mushrooms (such as cremini, beech, or shiitake), roughly chopped

4 slices bacon, sliced

3 large eggs

1 garlic clove, chopped

¾ cup whole milk

3 tablespoons unsalted butter, melted, divided

½ cup all-purpose flour

2 tablespoons cornstarch

Kosher salt

1 tablespoon fresh thyme, chopped

2 ounces Fontina or Cheddar cheese, shredded (about ½ cup)

1 scallion, thinly sliced

2 tablespoons chopped fresh flat-leaf parsley

ACTIVE TIME 25 min. | **TOTAL TIME** 1 hr. 10 min. | **SERVES** 4-6

1. Set the oven racks in the middle and upper positions. Heat the oven to 450°F. Place the mushrooms and bacon on a rimmed baking sheet and place on the top rack in the oven while preheating. Roast, stirring once, until the mushrooms are golden brown, 25 to 30 minutes. Place a 10-inch cast iron skillet on the middle rack and heat for 15 minutes.

2. Place the eggs and garlic in a blender. Process on high until frothy, 45 seconds. With the blender running, gradually add the milk and 2 tablespoons of the butter; stop blender. Add the flour, cornstarch and ¼ teaspoon salt; process 1 minute. Add the thyme.

3. Carefully add the remaining tablespoon butter to the heated skillet and swirl to coat. Immediately pour in the batter. Bake until golden brown and puffed, 14 to 16 minutes. Sprinkle with the cheese and bake until melted, 3 to 5 minutes.

4. Top with the mushroom mixture, scallions and parsley.

PER SERVING *About 351 calories, 24 g fat (11 g saturated fat), 15 g protein, 405 mg sodium, 21 g carbohydrates, 2 g fiber*

3/4 cup sweetened shredded coconut

1/4 cup panko breadcrumbs

2 scallions, finely chopped

1/2 cup all-purpose flour

1 large egg

8 small chicken cutlets (about 1 1/2 pounds)

Kosher salt and pepper

4 tablespoons olive oil, divided

◦ Coconut-Crusted Chicken Cutlets

ACTIVE TIME 20 min. | **TOTAL TIME** 20 min. | **SERVES** 4

1. In a shallow bowl, combine the coconut, panko and scallions. Place the flour in a second bowl, and in a third bowl, beat the egg with 1 tablespoon water.

2. Season the chicken cutlets with 1/2 teaspoon each salt and pepper. Dip each in flour, then egg, letting any excess drip off, then coat in the coconut mixture, pressing gently to help it adhere.

3. Heat 2 tablespoons of the oil in a large skillet on medium. Add half of the cutlets and cook until golden brown and cooked through, 3 to 4 minutes per side; transfer to a plate and wipe out the skillet. Repeat with the remaining oil and cutlets.

PER SERVING *About 455 calories, 22 g fat (8.5 g saturated fat), 39 g protein, 395 mg sodium, 25 g carbohydrates, 2 g fiber*

2 tablespoons olive oil, divided

2 medium onions, thinly sliced

Kosher salt and pepper

1 1/2 pounds sirloin steak, frozen for 2 hours

4 ounces sliced American or provolone cheese

4 hoagie or hero rolls, warmed and split

Sautéed mushrooms or peppers, for serving (optional)

Philly Cheesesteaks

ACTIVE TIME 25 min. | **TOTAL TIME** 25 min. | **SERVES** 4

1. Heat 1 tablespoon of the oil in a large skillet on medium. Add the onions and 1/4 teaspoon each salt and pepper and cook, covered, stirring occasionally, for 8 minutes. Uncover and cook, stirring occasionally, until golden brown and very tender, 6 to 8 minutes more; transfer to a bowl.

2. Meanwhile, slice the steak very thinly and season it with 1/2 teaspoon each salt and pepper.

3. Wipe out the skillet and heat the remaining tablespoon oil on medium-high. Cook the steak, tossing occasionally, until browned and cooked through, 3 to 4 minutes.

4. Lay the cheese over the steak, cover, and cook until the cheese melts, about 2 minutes. Remove from the heat and gently fold the cheese into the steak.

5. Form sandwiches with the rolls, steak mixture and onions. Top with mushrooms or peppers if desired.

PER SERVING *About 715 calories, 40 g fat (15 g saturated fat), 47 g protein, 445 mg sodium, 40 g carbohydrates, 3 g fiber*

5 tablespoons lime juice, plus lime wedges for serving

2 tablespoons reduced-sodium soy sauce

1 teaspoon sugar

4 tablespoons canola oil, divided

8 ounces tiny shiitake mushrooms or shiitake mushroom caps, sliced

4 scallions, thinly sliced

1 1-inch piece fresh ginger, peeled and cut into matchsticks

2 garlic cloves, thinly sliced

1 jalapeño, seeded and thinly sliced

4 cups cooked basmati rice

1 cup frozen shelled edamame, thawed

Chopped fresh cilantro, for topping

4 large eggs, fried to desired doneness (optional)

◄ Fried Rice

ACTIVE TIME 25 min. | **TOTAL TIME** 25 min. | **SERVES** 4

1. In a bowl, whisk together the lime juice, soy sauce, and sugar; set aside.

2. Heat a large, deep skillet on medium-high. Add 2 tablespoons of the oil, then the mushrooms, and cook, tossing, until just golden brown, 2 to 3 minutes; transfer to a plate.

3. Return the skillet to medium-high. Add the remaining 2 tablespoons oil, then the scallions, ginger, garlic and jalapeño. Cook, stirring, for 1 minute. Add the rice and edamame and cook, tossing, for 1 minute. Add the lime juice mixture along with the reserved mushrooms and toss to combine.

4. Sprinkle with cilantro and serve with lime wedges if desired. Top each serving with a fried egg if desired.

PER SERVING *About 540 calories, 23.5 g fat (3 g saturated fat), 39 g protein, 275 mg sodium, 71 g carbohydrates, 4 g fiber*

MAKE IT VEGAN **Omit eggs and sub in an extra cup of edamame to add more protein.**

2 tablespoons olive oil

2 pounds chicken legs

Kosher salt and ground black pepper

1 large onion, sliced

1 cup pitted green olives

¼ teaspoon red pepper flakes

1 preserved lemon, sliced

1 cinnamon stick

1 cup chicken broth

Chopped fresh flat-leaf parsley, for topping

Tunisian Skillet Chicken

ACTIVE TIME 15 min. | **TOTAL TIME** 30 min. | **SERVES** 4

1. Heat the oil in a large skillet on medium-high. Add the chicken, season with ½ teaspoon salt, and cook until golden brown, about 4 minutes per side. Transfer to a plate.

2. Add the onion, olives and red pepper flakes to the skillet and cook for 4 minutes. Stir in the preserved lemon, cinnamon and chicken broth, then return the chicken to the pan along with any juices.

3. Cover and cook on medium until the chicken is cooked through (165°F on an instant-read thermometer), about 15 minutes. Discard the cinnamon. To serve, sprinkle with parsley and black pepper.

PER SERVING *About 485 calories, 38 g fat (9 g saturated fat), 28 g protein, 1,085 mg sodium, 7 g carbohydrates, 2 g fiber*

3 tablespoons olive oil, divided

10 ounces cremini mushrooms, quartered

Kosher salt and pepper

1 large shallot, finely chopped

2 Gala apples, cored and cut into ½-inch-thick wedges

1 tablespoon unsalted butter

4 bone-in, skin-on chicken thighs (about 1½ pounds)

½ cup dry white wine

½ cup low-sodium chicken broth

6 thyme sprigs, plus more for serving

¼ cup heavy cream

1 tablespoon Dijon mustard

‹Chicken with Sautéed Apples & Mushrooms

ACTIVE TIME 30 min. | **TOTAL TIME** 30 min. | **SERVES** 4

1. Heat the oven to 375°F. Heat 2 tablespoons of the oil in a large oven-safe skillet on medium-high. Add the mushrooms and a pinch of salt and cook, tossing occasionally, for 5 minutes. Add the shallot and cook, stirring occasionally, until the mushrooms are golden brown, 2 to 3 minutes; transfer to a plate. Add the apples and butter to the skillet and cook, tossing occasionally, until beginning to turn golden brown, 2 to 3 minutes; transfer to a second plate and wipe the skillet clean.

2. Return the skillet to medium heat. Rub the chicken with the remaining tablespoon oil, season with ½ teaspoon each salt and pepper and cook, skin side down first, until browned, 8 to 10 minutes; drain excess fat. Turn the chicken skin side up, add the wine and cook for 1 minute, then add the broth and thyme. Return the apples to the skillet, transfer the skillet to the oven, and bake until the chicken is cooked through (165°F on an instant-read thermometer), 7 to 8 minutes.

3. Transfer the chicken and apples to a plate, discard the thyme and return the skillet to medium heat. Whisk in the cream and mustard, then fold in the mushroom mixture and cook until heated through, about 2 minutes. Serve with the chicken and apples and additional thyme if desired.

PER SERVING *About 475 calories, 34 g fat (11 g saturated fat), 26 g protein, 455 mg sodium, 19 g carbohydrates, 3 g fiber*

12 ounces thin spaghetti

4 cups low-sodium chicken broth

1 cup low-sodium marinara sauce

1 14½ ounce can petite diced tomatoes, drained

2 tablespoons olive oil

1 small onion, finely chopped

2 garlic cloves, finely chopped

½ cup torn basil leaves

Kosher salt and pepper

Grated Parmesan cheese, for topping

Spaghetti Marinara

ACTIVE TIME 20 min. | **TOTAL TIME** 20 min. | **SERVES** 4

1. Place the spaghetti in a large straight-sided skillet (it should lie flat on the bottom). Add the chicken broth, marinara, tomatoes and olive oil. Bring to a boil.

2. Add the onion and garlic to the skillet (it's okay if the liquid hasn't started boiling yet). Stir frequently until the liquid comes to a boil, then reduce the heat and simmer, stirring often, until the pasta is cooked, 6 to 10 minutes.

3. Stir in the basil, season with ¼ teaspoon each salt and pepper and serve with Parmesan.

PER SERVING *About 472 calories, 10.5 g fat (1.5 g saturated fat), 18 g protein, 406 mg sodium, 76 g carbohydrates, 5 g fiber*

3 tablespoons extra virgin olive oil

6 ounces rustic bread, torn into
¾-inch pieces

Kosher salt and pepper

2 garlic cloves, finely chopped

1 pound plum tomatoes, cut into
½-inch pieces

Small bunch basil, leaves torn, divided

1 pound large shrimp, peeled
and deveined

3 ounces mozzarella cheese,
shredded (about 1 cup)

3 tablespoons grated
Parmesan cheese

‹ Baked Shrimp Parmesan

ACTIVE TIME 25 min. | **TOTAL TIME** 40 min. | **SERVES** 4

1. Heat the oven to 425°F. Heat 2 tablespoons of the oil in a 12-inch oven-safe skillet on medium-low. Add the bread and toss in the oil to coat, then season with ¼ teaspoon each salt and pepper. Transfer the skillet to the oven and bake until the bread is golden brown and crisp, 8 to 10 minutes.

2. Transfer the bread to a plate. Add the remaining tablespoon oil and the garlic to the skillet. Cook, stirring, until the garlic starts to turn golden brown, about 1 minute. Add the tomatoes and ¼ teaspoon each salt and pepper and cook, tossing occasionally, until the juices start to release, 5 to 7 minutes. Fold in half of the basil.

3. Fold the shrimp and bread into the tomato mixture. Sprinkle with the mozzarella and Parmesan. Bake until the shrimp are opaque throughout and the cheese is golden brown and bubbling, 14 to 16 minutes. Scatter the remaining basil on top and serve immediately.

PER SERVING *About 348 calories, 17.5 g fat (5 g saturated fat), 33 g protein, 1,089 mg sodium, 23 g carbohydrates, 2 g fiber*

4 tablespoons unsalted butter

¼ cup all-purpose flour

3 cups whole milk, warmed

Kosher salt and pepper

8 ounces mezze rigatoni

8 ounces extra-sharp Cheddar
cheese, coarsely shredded

1 10-ounce package frozen butternut
squash cubes, thawed

3 ounces baby spinach (about 3 cups)

4 ounces potato chips (about 3 cups),
crushed

2 tablespoons finely chopped
fresh chives

2 tablespoons finely grated
Parmesan cheese

≡ QUICK & EASY ≡

Skillet Mac & Cheese

ACTIVE TIME 20 min. | **TOTAL TIME** 30 min. | **SERVES** 4

1. Heat the oven to 350°F. Melt the butter in a deep 12-inch oven-safe skillet on medium. Once the butter is foaming, add the flour and whisk until smooth. Gradually whisk in the milk a little at a time, making sure the mixture is smooth before adding more liquid. Add 1 cup water and ½ teaspoon each salt and pepper. Bring to a simmer, stirring occasionally.

2. Immediately add the pasta and cook, stirring, for 1 minute. Cover the skillet, transfer to the oven and bake until the pasta is just cooked, 12 to 14 minutes.

3. Remove from the oven and heat the broiler. Fold the Cheddar into the pasta until melted and smooth, then fold in the squash and spinach. Sprinkle the potato chips, chives and Parmesan on top and broil until golden brown, 1 to 2 minutes.

PER SERVING *About 878 calories, 47 g fat (24.5 g saturated fat), 33 g protein, 919 mg sodium, 80 g carbohydrates, 4 g fiber*

Spiced Beef Hot Pot

2 tablespoons extra virgin olive oil, divided

2 pounds lean beef chuck, trimmed and cut into 1½-inch pieces

Kosher salt and pepper

4 medium carrots, cut into 2-inch pieces

1 medium onion, sliced

¼ teaspoon ground cinnamon

¼ teaspoon ground allspice

2 bay leaves

2 tablespoons tomato paste

1 tablespoon all-purpose flour

½ cup dry red wine

1 14-ounce can diced tomatoes

2½ pounds russet potatoes (about 3 medium), peeled and sliced ⅓ inch thick

2 tablespoons unsalted butter, melted, divided

Chopped fresh flat-leaf parsley, for topping (optional)

ACTIVE TIME 35 min. | **TOTAL TIME** 2 hr. 20 min. | **SERVES** 4-6

1. Heat the oven to 325°F. Heat 1 tablespoon of the oil in a 12-inch oven-safe skillet on medium-high. Season the beef with ½ teaspoon each salt and pepper. Working in two batches, brown the beef on all sides, 5 to 6 minutes; transfer to a bowl.

2. Reduce the heat to low, add the remaining tablespoon oil along with the carrots and onion and cook, stirring occasionally, for 5 minutes. Return the beef to the pan (along with any juices) and add the cinnamon, allspice and bay leaves. Cook, stirring, for 1 minute. Add the tomato paste and cook, stirring, for 1 minute.

3. Sprinkle the flour over the top and cook, stirring, for 1 minute. Add the wine and bring to a simmer, scraping up any brown bits, then add the tomatoes (including their liquid).

4. Return to a simmer, then remove from the heat. Arrange the potatoes in a spiral on top of the beef and vegetable mixture, slightly overlapping them. Brush with half of the butter and sprinkle with ¼ teaspoon each salt and pepper. Cover the skillet, transfer to the oven and bake until the beef and potatoes are tender, 1½ to 1¾ hours. Remove from the oven.

5. Heat the broiler. Brush the potatoes with the remaining butter and broil until golden brown, 5 to 7 minutes. Sprinkle with parsley if desired.

PER SERVING About 741 calories, 30 g fat (12 g saturated fat), 55 g protein, 803 mg sodium, 64 g carbohydrates, 7 g fiber

TIP Switch up this recipe by substituting celery root for half the potatoes. Peel and slice as thinly as the potatoes and arrange in alternating concentric circles.

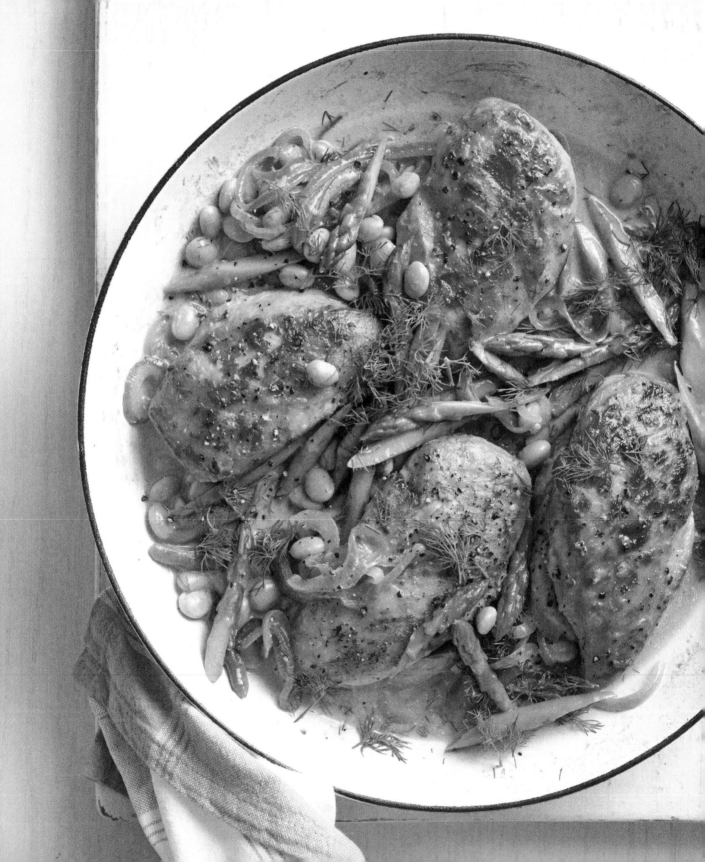

3 tablespoons all-purpose flour

Kosher salt and pepper

4 boneless, skinless chicken breasts

2 tablespoons olive oil

1 small red onion, chopped

1 garlic clove, finely chopped

½ cup dry white wine

1 cup low-sodium chicken broth

1 pound asparagus, cut into
    1-inch pieces

1 cup frozen edamame, thawed

2 tablespoons chopped fresh dill

1 tablespoon sour cream

1 tablespoon lemon juice

Steamed new potatoes or crusty
    bread, for serving (optional)

Spring Chicken with Asparagus & Edamame

ACTIVE TIME 20 min. | **TOTAL TIME** 30 min. | **SERVES** 4

1. In a shallow bowl or pie dish, whisk together the flour and ½ teaspoon each salt and pepper. Coat the chicken breasts in the flour mixture.

2. Heat the oil in a large skillet on medium-high and cook the chicken breasts until golden brown on one side, 4 to 6 minutes. Turn the chicken, add the onion and garlic and cook, stirring the onion and garlic occasionally, for 3 minutes.

3. Add the wine to the skillet and simmer, scraping up any brown bits, until reduced by half, 1 to 2 minutes. Add the broth, return to a boil, then reduce the heat and simmer until the chicken is cooked through, 5 to 6 minutes more.

4. Two minutes before the chicken is done, add the asparagus and edamame to the skillet and cook, stirring occasionally, until just tender.

5. Remove from the heat and stir in the dill, sour cream and lemon juice. Serve with potatoes or crusty bread if desired.

PER SERVING *About 361 calories, 14 g fat (2.5 g saturated fat), 44 g protein, 477 mg sodium, 15 g carbohydrates, 15 g fiber*

TIP **Switch up this recipe by substituting 4 small boneless pork chops for the chicken. Cook until golden brown on one side, 3 to 4 minutes, then turn, add the onion and garlic and cook as directed.**

2 12-ounce strip steaks (each about 1½ inches thick)

Kosher salt and pepper

3 tablespoons olive oil, divided

4 skin-on garlic cloves, plus 2 cloves finely chopped, divided

1 rosemary sprig, plus 1 teaspoon chopped fresh rosemary, divided

12 ounces assorted mushrooms (such as oyster, shiitake, and cremini), quartered

½ cup dry white wine

1 tablespoon Dijon mustard

1 bunch spinach, thick stems discarded and leaves roughly chopped (about 6 cups)

½ cup crème fraîche or sour cream

Steak with Creamy Mushrooms & Spinach

ACTIVE TIME 20 min. | **TOTAL TIME** 35 min. | **SERVES** 4

1. Heat the oven to 425°F. Season the steaks with salt and pepper. Heat 1 tablespoon of the oil in a medium-size cast iron skillet on medium-high. Add the steaks, skin-on garlic and rosemary sprig. Cook, turning once, until browned, 4 to 8 minutes.

2. Transfer the skillet to the oven and roast the steaks to desired doneness, 3 to 6 minutes for medium. Transfer the steaks to a cutting board, loosely tent with foil and let rest at least 10 minutes before slicing.

3. Return the skillet to medium-high heat (make sure to keep an oven mitt on the handle). Add the mushrooms and the remaining 2 tablespoons oil. Season with salt. Cook, stirring occasionally, until the mushrooms are softened and starting to brown, 6 to 8 minutes. Add the chopped garlic and the chopped rosemary and cook, stirring, until fragrant, 1 minute.

4. Add wine and mustard. Cook, stirring, until thickened, 30 seconds. Transfer the mushrooms to a plate. Add the spinach to the skillet and cook, tossing, until beginning to wilt, 1 to 2 minutes. Remove from the heat and stir in the crème fraîche and mushrooms. Season with salt and pepper. Serve the sauce with the sliced steak.

PER SERVING *About 640 calories, 48 g fat (19 g saturated fat), 40 g protein, 594 mg sodium, 10 g carbohydrates, 3 g fiber*

TIP When prepping shitake mushrooms, separate the caps from the stems (which can be tough). Save the stems and drop into broth or soups for an extra hit of flavor.

2 tablespoons extra virgin olive oil

4 garlic cloves, finely chopped

2 teaspoons vegetable bouillon base (we used Better Than Bouillon)

12 ounces orecchiette or other short pasta

2 teaspoons fresh thyme leaves

1 14-ounce can small white beans, rinsed and drained

2 cups baby spinach

½ cup finely grated Parmesan cheese

Freshly ground black pepper

QUICK & EASY

‹ Orecchiette with White Beans & Spinach

ACTIVE TIME 15 min. | **TOTAL TIME** 25 min. | **SERVES** 4

1. Heat the oil and garlic in a large deep skillet over medium heat until the garlic is lightly golden brown, about 2 minutes. Remove from the heat, add 4 cups of water and whisk in the bouillon base.

2. Add the orecchiette and the thyme and bring to a boil. Reduce the heat and simmer, stirring frequently, until the orecchiette is firm-tender, 10 to 12 minutes.

3. Fold in the beans, spinach, Parmesan and ½ teaspoon pepper and cook until the beans are heated through, about 2 minutes.

PER SERVING *500 calories, 11.5 g fat (2.5 g saturated fat), 21 g protein, 678 mg sodium, 84 g carbohydrates, 8 g fiber*

4 teaspoons olive oil, divided

2 thin slices red onion

12 ounces sweet Italian sausage

2 ounces extra-sharp Cheddar cheese, coarsely shredded

4 large eggs

4 English muffins, split and toasted

6 sweet piquante peppers, such as Peppadews, sliced

¼ cup chopped fresh flat-leaf parsley

QUICK & EASY

Sausage & Egg Sandwiches

ACTIVE TIME 15 min. | **TOTAL TIME** 15 min. | **SERVES** 4

1. Heat 2 teaspoons of the olive oil in large cast iron skillet on medium. Add the onion and cook for 3 minutes. Remove the sausage from its casings and, with wet hands, shape it into four ¼-inch-thick patties. Add to the skillet with the onion and increase the heat to medium-high. Flip the onion and cook until just tender, 2 to 3 minutes more, then flip the patties, which should be browned.

2. Separate the onion slices into rings and arrange on top of the patties, then top with the cheese and continue cooking until the sausage is cooked through, 2 to 3 minutes more.

3. Meanwhile, heat the remaining 2 teaspoons olive oil in large nonstick skillet on medium and cook the eggs to desired doneness, 4 to 5 minutes for runny yolks. Top the bottom halves of the English muffins with sausage, then eggs, piquante peppers and parsley.

PER SERVING *480 calories, 29 g fat (10 g saturated fat), 24 g protein, 785 mg sodium, 30 g carbohydrates, 2 g fiber*

TIP Pickled peppers add a sweet-hot kick that pairs well with the rich sausage, but for a milder contrast, sub in roasted red peppers instead.

Chapter 5

The Air Fryer

What if we told you there was a machine that could "fry" foods into light and crispy perfection with little to no oil? Meet the air fryer. With the turn of a dial or press of a button, this trendy tool can fry up everything from bite-size appetizers to weeknight main dishes in minutes—with all the flavor of fried favorites.

What's the difference between an air fryer and a deep fryer?

Air fryers bake food and circulate hot air with a high power fan, turning out crispy results. They are similar to mini convection ovens but work in a fraction of the time it would take your oven without heating up the house (a serious summertime game changer). Deep fryers cook food in a vat of oil that has been heated up to a specific temperature. Both cook food quickly, but an air fryer requires practically zero preheat time while a deep fryer can take upwards of 10 minutes. Air fryers also require little to no oil; deep fryers require a lot, some of which absorbs into the food. Food comes out crispy and juicy in both appliances, but it won't necessarily taste the same. Deep fried foods are sometimes coated in batter and cook differently in an air fryer versus a deep fryer. Battered foods need to be sprayed with oil before cooking in an air fryer to help them color and get crispy, while the hot oil soaks into the batter in a deep fryer. Flour-based batters and wet batters don't cook well in an air fryer, but light breadings come out great.

What can you cook in an air fryer?

Air fryers are fast, and they can be used to heat frozen foods or cook all sorts of fresh food like chicken, steak, pork chops, salmon and vegetables. Most meats require no added oil because they're already so juicy: Just season them with salt and your favorite herbs and spices. Stick to dry seasonings—less moisture leads to crispier results. If you want to baste meats with barbecue sauce or honey, wait until the last couple of minutes of cooking.

Lean cuts of meat Meat or foods with little or no fat require oil to brown and crisp up. Brush boneless chicken breasts and pork chops with a bit of oil before seasoning. Vegetable oil or canola oil is usually recommended due to its neutral taste and higher smoke point, meaning it can stand up to the high heat in an air fryer.

Vegetables Toss vegetables in oil before air frying. We recommend sprinkling them with salt too, but use a little less than you're used to: The crispy, air fried bits pack a lot of flavor. We love air frying broccoli florets, Brussels sprouts and baby potato halves. They come out so crispy! Butternut squash, sweet potatoes and beets all seem to get sweeter and green beans and peppers take no time at all.

Are there other benefits to using an air fryer?
Another great part of air frying is the cleanup. Most air fryer baskets and racks are dishwasher-safe. For the ones that are not dishwasher-safe, we suggest a good bottle brush. It'll get into all the nooks and crannies—that promote air circulation!—without driving you nuts.

How to Choose an Air Fryer

::::::::::::::::::::::::::

Thinking about adding an air fryer to your kitchen counter? First consider whether you need a new appliance. Toaster ovens, microwaves, pressure cookers and even full-sized ovens have started to incorporate an air fry option into their designs, so investing in a multifunctional appliance might be a better value (that takes up less space!). If you do decide an air fryer is the way to go, here are some questions to guide your search.

What size do I need?
How many people are you cooking for at one time? The smallest air fryers (1.2 liters) are good for 1 to 2 people, while the medium sizes (3–4 liters) are good for 2 to 3 people and the largest (6 liters or more) are good for 4 to 6.

What style works best for me?
Most air fryer models have a drawer that pulls out, with a metal basket inside. Just toss your food in a bowl with a couple tablespoons of oil, place the oil-coated food in the basket and then set the temperature and the timer to cook. Basket-style air fryers are good for small quantities and foods that are easy to shake, like fries and vegetables; air fryer ovens are a bit bigger and can air fry food on multiple shelves, but they require more monitoring and often need to be rotated during cooking; air fryer toaster ovens can perform multiple cooking functions, including air fry. Air fryers with baskets instead of shelves are preferable because they cook more evenly.

What is my price point?
Digital air fryers tend to cost more than mechanical air fryers, as do stainless steel versus plastic. Think about the features and size that will work best for you to narrow down your choices. Then read reviews for those models that fall into your ideal price point before making your final decision. Know that stand-alone air fryers range in price from $40 for small compact models to $400 for large air fryer toaster ovens.

TOP-TESTED AIR FRYERS

We've tested more than 30 air fryers in the Good Housekeeping Institute Kitchen Appliances Lab, including traditional basket-style air fryers, air fryer ovens, air fryer toaster ovens and even several microwaves and multicookers with air fry capabilities. We also cook with them quite regularly and have developed countless recipes.

When we test air fryers, we evaluate their performance and ease of use by air frying frozen and fresh French fries and chicken wings. We don't test baked goods like cake because baked goods benefit from an even distribution of gentle heat and most air fryers don't have heating elements on the bottom in addition to the top (though fruit crumbles and doughnuts come out great!). We score the food on its crispiness, juiciness and evenness, and we consider details like how quickly it cooks, how helpful the user guide is and whether the machine is loud. We also evaluate features like the control panel, temperature range and whether the accessories are dishwasher-safe.

Our top performers air fried food to a crispy texture with a moist interior and were a cinch to use with large, easy-to-read controls that barely required the owner's manual.

**SCAN FOR
MORE AIR FRYER
LAB REVIEWS**

BEST OVERALL
5½-quart Ninja Air Fryer Max XL
The Fryer Max was the top performer in our traditional, basket-style air fryer test. It scored the highest marks across the board for ease of use, thanks to its intuitive, easy-to-read buttons and clear owner's manual. During our tests, the air fryer basket slid in and out easily, which made handling a breeze. We're fans of the basket's removable tray and slick, ceramic-coated interior, which makes it nonstick. The tray also fits snugly and securely on the bottom of the basket so you don't have to worry about it falling out when you turn the food out onto a plate. Both are dishwasher-safe and easy to clean, even if you choose to hand wash.

In addition to being easy to use, the Ninja Air Fryer Max XL scored the highest in performance. It produced crispy and evenly cooked frozen fries, homemade fries and chicken wings that were moist on the inside. The model we tested comes with a broiling rack for even quicker and juicier results—and it's a fast way to create melty cheese. It also features several cook settings, including max crisp and air broil (which reach 450°F) and dehydrate (which reaches a low of 105°F). The different settings are programmed with unique maximum and minimum temperatures, so you can select them to achieve different cooking results. Another unique feature is the timer, which counts down to the second. For a larger capacity, consider the Ninja Foodi 6-in-1 2-Basket Air Fryer. It performs as well as the Air Fryer Max XL with more versatility.

Air Fryer Care

::::::::::::::::::::::::::::

Cleaning the Fryer Basket and Pan

1. Many models have dishwasher-safe parts. To wash by hand, fill the pan with hot water and add a few drops of dishwashing soap. Allow the pan, with the basket inside, to soak for ten minutes.

2. After ten minutes, wipe the basket walls and bottom, plus the pan, with a moist dish cloth or a nonabrasive sponge.

3. Allow both the basket and the pan to air-dry before putting them back into the device.

Cleaning the Appliance

Clean the outside of the air fryer with a moist dish cloth, as well as the walls of the interior cavity that hold the fryer basket. Food residues stuck to the heating element inside may be removed with a nonabrasive sponge or a soft-bristle brush and wiped dry with a paper towel. Avoid steel wool or hard-bristle brushes, as these tools can damage the coating on the heating element.

CHEESY-STUFFED CHICKEN WITH GREEN BEANS 157

Cooking Tips for Best Results

Before you start air frying, be sure to follow these simple steps for the best results:

1. **Don't overcrowd the fryer basket.** This ensures a light and crispy exterior.

2. **Begin to air fry your food within a few minutes of tossing in the oil.**

3. **Use oil sparingly.** Naturally fatty foods like chicken wings and bone-in pork chops don't need extra oil—just season with salt or your favorite spices before air frying.

4. **Say no to stacking.** For the quickest and most even results, arrange foods in a single layer, allowing enough room for foods to be tossed or shaken easily during cooking.

5. **Use small pieces.** For quicker cooking and the tastiest (and juiciest!) outcome, cut large steaks into two to four pieces and chop vegetables into bite-size pieces.

6. **Take care with quick-cooking ingredients.** When air frying different ingredients at the same time, put faster-cooking ingredients in the air fryer later in the process, or cut them into larger pieces so they'll cook at the same rate as sturdier ingredients like potatoes.

7. **Gently shake.** Smaller ingredients in the fryer basket will need a little shake halfway through cooking (or every 5 to 10 minutes) to help them cook evenly and enhance their crispy texture.

8. **Don't add oil.** Prepackaged frozen foods don't need additional oil before being air fried.

9. **Use caution.** When preparing highly greasy foods (like sausages) in the air fryer, use caution as excessive fat dripping into the pan can cause smoking.

10. **It's okay to pull the basket out.** At any time throughout the cooking cycle you may pull out the basket to check on the progress—most models will automatically shut off while the basket is out and resume when it's pushed back in. If food isn't sufficiently fried when the timer goes off, set the timer for a few extra minutes and continue cooking.

11. **Use caution with hot tools.** Always set the basket, pan and any accessories on a heat-resistant surface when frying is complete, as these tools get very hot during the cooking process.

12. **Use tongs.** When air frying larger or delicate foods, use tongs to lift them out of the fryer basket. Otherwise, you can often turn the food out directly onto a serving bowl or platter. (Be careful with models that have a removable tray. The tray doesn't always stay put when turned upside down.)

13. **Pour out excess oil after each batch.** If you've been prepping fatty ingredients and excess oil has collected in the bottom of the basket, pour it out before cooking anything else.

Air Fryer Cooking Guide

Looking for a fast dinner that you can make with foods you have on hand already? This guide provides a everything you need at a glance, making it easy to air fry meals in a matter of minutes. From favorites like juicy chicken breasts to perfectly cooked fish fillets, this food temperature chart with tips will set you up for success when cooking with your air fryer.

AIR FRYER CHEAT SHEET

FOOD	TEMPERATURE	TIME	TIP
Meat and Seafood			
Chicken breasts (6 ounces each)	380°F	10–15 minutes	Brush with oil and season; flip halfway through cooking
Chicken wings (split, 1 pound)	400°F	20–25 minutes	Toss with seasoning
Chicken thighs (bone-in)	400°F	15–20 minutes	Season and arrange skin side up
Chicken drumsticks	350°F	20–25 minutes	
Chicken nuggets	400°F	8–12 minutes	Shake halfway through cooking
Pork chops (bone-in, 1 inch thick)	400°F	10–15 minutes	Season and flip halfway through cooking
Steak (1 inch thick)	400°F	10–15 minutes	Season and flip halfway through cooking
Hamburger	400°F	8–12 minutes	
Meatballs	350°F	10–15 minutes	
Fish fillets (1 inch thick, 6 ounces each)	400°F	8–10 minutes	Brush with oil and season
Shellfish	350°F	7–15 minutes	

FOOD	TEMPERATURE	TIME	TIP
Frozen Foods			
Frozen fries (1 pound)	400°F	15–20 minutes	Shake twice during cooking
Frozen snacks (spring rolls, onion rings, etc.)	400°F	8–14 minutes or until hot	Shake halfway through cooking
Vegetables			
Butternut squash (cut into 1-inch pieces)	400°F	12–15 minutes	Toss with oil and season; shake the basket halfway through cooking
Brussels sprouts (halved)	400°F	10–15 minutes	Toss with oil and season; shake the basket twice during cooking
Sweet potatoes (cut into 1-inch wedges)	400°F	12–15 minutes	Toss with oil and season; shake the basket halfway through cooking
Homemade fries	400°F	15–24 minutes	Shake halfway through cooking
Mixed vegetables	350°F	8–12 minutes	Shake halfway through cooking
Baked potato	400°F	25 minutes or until tender	Pierce skin of potato before cooking
Potato wedges	350°F	18–25 minutes	Shake halfway through cooking

1 tablespoon red wine vinegar

2 tablespoons olive oil, divided

1 tablespoon capers, chopped

1 scallion, finely chopped

Ground black pepper

1 pint grape tomatoes

Kosher salt

1 pound skinless salmon fillets, cut into 1½-inch pieces

1 tablespoon chopped flat-leaf parsley

½ cup labneh or Greek yogurt

4 naans or flatbreads, warmed

2 cups baby arugula or kale

Sliced scallions, for topping

Crumbed feta, for topping (optional)

Salmon & Tomato Flatbreads

ACTIVE TIME 15 min. | **TOTAL TIME** 15 min. | **SERVES** 4

1. In a small bowl, combine red wine vinegar, 1 tablespoon of the olive oil, capers, scallion and ¼ teaspoon pepper; set aside.

2. Heat the air fryer to 400°F. In a bowl, toss the grape tomatoes, the remaining olive oil and ¼ teaspoon each kosher salt and pepper. Season the salmon with ¼ teaspoon each salt and pepper.

3. Place the salmon in a single layer on one side of the air fryer and add the tomatoes to the remaining space (piling them is great). Air fry until the salmon is barely opaque throughout, about 6 minutes.

4. Transfer the tomatoes to a bowl with the vinegar-scallion mixture and toss to combine, then toss with the parsley.

5. Spread labneh or Greek yogurt on naan or flatbread, top with the salmon and baby arugula or kale. Spoon the tomato mixture on top. Sprinkle with sliced scallions and crumbled feta if desired.

PER SERVING *About 490 calories, 25 g fat (9 g saturated), 41 g protein, 750 mg sodium, 30 g carbohydrates, 10 g fiber*

1 plum tomato, seeded and chopped

2 tablespoons extra virgin olive oil

1 tablespoon chopped fresh basil

1 tablespoon capers, drained
and chopped

1 teaspoon lemon juice

Kosher salt

4 ounces fresh mozzarella
cheese, sliced

4 slices firm white bread,
crusts trimmed

1 egg

2 tablespoons all-purpose flour

½ cup panko breadcrumbs

3 tablespoons grated
Parmesan cheese

Olive oil in mister

Mozzarella en Carrozza

ACTIVE TIME 25 min. | **TOTAL TIME** 30 min. | **SERVES** 4

1. Mix together the tomato, oil, basil, capers, lemon juice and ⅛ teaspoon salt. Set the tomato dressing aside.

2. Place the mozzarella between the bread slices, making 2 sandwiches. Cut each sandwich in half diagonally.

3. Beat the egg in a shallow dish. Mix together the flour and ¼ teaspoon salt in another dish. Mix together the panko and Parmesan in another dish. Dip the sandwich halves, one at a time, into the flour mixture to coat on all sides. Shake off the excess flour. Dip in the egg, and then in the panko mixture, pressing the panko to stick.

4. Heat the air fryer to 390°F. Spray the air fryer basket with olive oil. Spray the sandwiches on all sides with olive oil and arrange in the basket. Air fry for 5 minutes or until crisp and browned, turning once with tongs.

5. Cut each sandwich in half, making 8 triangles. Serve while hot with the tomato vinaigrette.

PER SERVING *About 295 calories, 18 g fat (7 g saturated fat), 11 g protein, 468 mg sodium, 23 g carbohydrates, 1 g fiber*

TIP The sandwiches can also be made with deli-sliced mozzarella cheese, using 2 ounces per sandwich (about 3 slices). Don't trim the crusts first, however. Trim after assembling, in case the cheese needs to be trimmed, too. Fresh mozzarella leaked slightly; the deli-sliced mozzarella did not.

2 pounds chicken wings, tips removed

Kosher salt

Sauce of your choice (see below)

Chicken Wings

ACTIVE TIME 10 min. | **TOTAL TIME** 50 min. | **SERVES** 6

1. Season the wings with ⅛ teaspoon salt.

2. Heat the air fryer to 400°F. Place half of the wings at a time in the basket and air fry until the skin is browned and the chicken is cooked through, about 15 minutes, turning with tongs halfway through cooking. Combine both batches in the air fryer and cook 4 minutes more. Transfer to a large bowl and toss with sauce until evenly coated. Serve immediately.

PER SERVING *(4 pieces, without sauce) About 180 calories, 12 g fat (4 g saturated fat), 17 g protein, 109 mg sodium, 0 g carbohydrates, 0 g fiber*

Fun Flavors

SESAME TERIYAKI SAUCE
In a large bowl, whisk together 3 tablespoons teriyaki sauce, 2 tablespoons rice vinegar, 1 tablespoon dark brown sugar and 2 teaspoons sesame oil; toss with hot cooked wings and 2 tablespoons sesame seeds.

SWEET 'N' STICKY THAI WINGS
In a medium bowl, combine ½ cup Thai sweet chili sauce, 2 teaspoons lime zest and 1 teaspoon fish sauce. Toss with hot cooked wings and sprinkle on ⅓ cup french-fried onions.

BUFFALO WINGS
In small saucepan, melt 3 tablespoons unsalted butter on medium. Whisk in ¼ cup cayenne pepper sauce and 2 tablespoons distilled white vinegar. Toss with hot cooked wings and serve with ranch dressing for dipping.

HOT CARIBBEAN WINGS
In small saucepan, combine 2 cups mango nectar, 2 teaspoons habanero hot sauce, pinch allspice and ⅛ teaspoon each kosher salt and pepper. Simmer until reduced by half, 8 minutes. Stir in 2 teaspoons fresh lime juice. Toss with hot cooked wings and sprinkle with chopped cilantro.

3 tablespoons fish sauce, divided

2 tablespoons lime juice, divided

1 tablespoon plus 1 teaspoon packed
   brown sugar, divided

4 cloves garlic, 2 pressed and
   2 thinly sliced

2 pounds chicken wings

½ pound shishito peppers

2 tablespoons plus 2 teaspoons
   canola oil

Kosher salt

1 small red chile, thinly sliced

Chopped cilantro and torn basil,
   for serving

Garlicky Wings & Shishito Peppers

ACTIVE TIME 20 min. | **TOTAL TIME** 25 min. | **SERVES** 4

1. In large bowl, whisk together 2 tablespoons fish sauce, 1 tablespoon lime juice and 1 tablespoon brown sugar to dissolve, then stir in pressed garlic and toss with wings. Refrigerate for at least 1 hour and up to 3 hours.

2. Heat the air fryer to 400°F. Transfer the wings to the air fryer and discard the marinade. Set the timer to 15 minutes, press Start and cook for 8 minutes.

3. In a small bowl, toss the shishito peppers with 2 teaspoons oil and ¼ teaspoon salt. Flip the wings, scatter shishito peppers around the wings and continue cooking until the wings are cooked through and the peppers are browned in spots, 7 minutes more. Transfer to a platter.

4. Meanwhile, combine 2 tablespoons oil and sliced garlic in a small bowl and microwave in 30-second intervals until sizzling. Remove from the microwave and stir in the chile, and the remaining lime juice, fish sauce and brown sugar. Spoon over the wings and peppers and sprinkle with the herbs.

PER SERVING *About 389 calories, 27.5 g fat (6 g saturated fat), 28 g protein, 821 mg sodium, 8 g carbohydrates, 2 g fiber*

TIP No air fryer? Fire up the grill instead! Heat grill to low. Place the wings, bone sides down, on the grill and cook, covered, for 10 minutes. Flip and continue grilling until cooked through, 10 to 15 minutes more. Grill the shishitos on medium-high, flipping once, until charred, 4 to 6 minutes total.

½ cup plain yogurt

1 tablespoon lemon juice

1 tablespoon paprika

½ tablespoon grated peeled
fresh ginger

2 garlic cloves, grated

1 teaspoon garam masala

½ teaspoon ground turmeric

½ teaspoon ground coriander

¼ teaspoon cayenne

4 small chicken legs, each split
into 2 parts

1 tablespoon olive oil, plus more
for misting or brushing

Kosher salt and pepper

2 small red onions, cut into
½-inch-thick wedges

Lemon wedges and fresh cilantro,
for serving

◂ Tandoori Chicken

ACTIVE TIME 20 min. | **TOTAL TIME** 55 min. | **SERVES** 4

1. In a medium bowl, whisk together the yogurt, lemon juice, paprika, ginger, garlic, garam masala, turmeric, coriander and cayenne. Add the chicken, turn to coat, and let sit 20 minutes (and up to 4 hours).

2. Heat the air fryer to 400°F. Coat the air fryer basket with oil. Remove the chicken from the marinade, season with ½ teaspoon salt and arrange, skin side up, in the basket. Air fry for 12 minutes.

3. Toss the onions with 1 tablespoon oil and ¼ teaspoon each salt and pepper and scatter around the chicken pieces. Air fry until the chicken is cooked through and the onions are golden brown and tender, 8 to 12 minutes more.

4. Transfer to a platter along with lemon wedges and sprinkle with cilantro if desired.

PER SERVING *About 440 calories, 23.5 g fat (6 g saturated fat), 48 g protein, 565 mg sodium, 7 g carbohydrates, 2 g fiber*

---

5 tablespoons light mayonnaise,
divided

1 teaspoon reduced-sodium soy sauce

1 large egg white

2 scallions, thinly sliced, divided

½ cup panko breadcrumbs, divided

8 ounces lump crabmeat, picked over

Oil, for misting or brushing

2 tablespoons seasoned rice vinegar

1 teaspoon sesame oil

½ teaspoon grated peeled
fresh ginger

3 cups shredded red cabbage

≡ QUICK & EASY ≡

Crab Cakes with Gingery Slaw

ACTIVE TIME 20 min. | **TOTAL TIME** 30 min. | **SERVES** 2

1. In a small bowl, whisk 2 tablespoons mayonnaise with the soy sauce; set the soy mayonnaise aside for serving.

2. In a medium bowl, mix together the egg white, half of the scallions, 2 tablespoons panko and the remaining 3 tablespoons mayonnaise. Add the crab and mix to combine. Shape into four 3-inch patties. Coat the patties with the remaining panko, pressing to help adhere.

3. Heat the air fryer to 400°F. Spray or brush the air fryer basket with oil. Spray or brush both sides of the crab cakes with oil. Air fry until the crab cakes are golden brown and cooked through, 10 minutes, turning once.

4. Meanwhile, in a large bowl, combine the vinegar, sesame oil, ginger and remaining scallions. Add the cabbage and toss to coat. Serve the slaw with the crab cakes and soy mayonnaise.

PER SERVING *About 390 calories, 17 g fat (3 g saturated fat), 26 g protein, 1,292 mg sodium, 34 g carbohydrates, 3 g fiber*

1/3 cup mayonnaise

2 tablespoons milk

1 teaspoon chili powder

1/4 teaspoon garlic powder

1 1/2 cups panko breadcrumbs

4 teaspoons canola or vegetable oil,
plus more for misting or brushing

Kosher salt

1 pound skinless mahimahi or tilapia
fillets, cut into 3-inch-long by
1-inch-wide strips

Small flour tortillas

Toppings of your choice (see below)

Crispy Fish Tacos

ACTIVE TIME 20 min. | **TOTAL TIME** 30 min. | **SERVES** 4

1. In a small bowl, whisk together the mayonnaise, milk, chili powder and garlic powder. On a plate, mix the panko with the oil and 1/2 teaspoon salt.

2. Working with a few strips at a time, toss the fish in the mayonnaise mixture to coat and then in the panko, pressing to help adhere. Place the coated fish strips on a baking sheet.

3. Heat the air fryer to 390°F. Spray or brush the air fryer basket with oil. In two batches, arrange the fish with space between the strips and stack strips perpendicularly in second layer. Air fry until cooked, 4 to 5 minutes per batch.

4. Serve in flour tortillas with your choice of toppings (below).

PER SERVING *(fish only) About 370 calories, 19 g fat (3 g saturated fat), 24 g protein, 525 mg sodium, 23 g carbohydrates, 1 g fiber*

Fun Flavors

PINEAPPLE & RED PEPPER SLAW
In a bowl, toss 1/4 large pineapple (cut into matchsticks; about 1 cup) and 1 small red pepper (thinly sliced) with 1 tablespoon olive oil, 1 teaspoon lime zest and 1/4 teaspoon salt; fold in 2 scallions (sliced into 3-inch matchsticks).

CITRUSY RADISHES
In a bowl, whisk together 1 tablespoon each orange juice and lemon juice and 1/4 teaspoon each ground cumin, kosher salt and pepper. Toss with 6 very thinly sliced radishes and 1/4 small sweet onion (thinly sliced). Fold in 1/4 cup chopped fresh cilantro.

CABBAGE SLAW
In a bowl, whisk together 2 tablespoons each sour cream and lime juice, 1/4 teaspoon salt and 1/8 teaspoon cayenne. Toss with 2 cups shredded green or red cabbage. Let stand, tossing often, for 10 minutes. Stir in 1 sliced scallion and 2 tablespoons chopped fresh cilantro.

2 large eggs, divided

1 cup ricotta cheese

1 cup roughly chopped baby spinach

1 cup chopped fresh basil

¼ cup finely chopped sundried tomatoes (about 9)

¼ teaspoon red pepper flakes

Kosher salt

2 refrigerated rolled pie crusts (from 15-ounce box)

Sesame seeds, for topping

◄ Spinach & Cheese Breakfast Pockets

ACTIVE TIME 20 min. | **TOTAL TIME** 1 hr. 20 min. | **SERVES** 8

1. In a small bowl, whisk 1 egg with 1 tablespoon water; set aside.

2. In a medium bowl, combine the ricotta, spinach, basil, sundried tomatoes, red pepper flakes, remaining egg and ¼ teaspoon salt.

3. Unroll the pie crusts and cut each into 4 wedges. Divide the ricotta mixture among the wedges (about 3 tablespoons for each), placing the ricotta on one side, ½ inch from the edges. Fold the dough over the filling and press the edges with a fork to seal.

4. Brush the tops with egg mixture and sprinkle with sesame seeds. Air fry at 380°F in batches (2 at a time) until golden brown, 10 to 12 minutes.

PER SERVING *About 285 calories, 8 g fat (8 g saturated fat), 8 g protein, 370 mg sodium, 27 g carbohydrates, 1 g fiber*

1½ pounds cod fillet

3 large egg whites, beaten

6 ounces salt-and-vinegar potato chips, finely crushed

Olive oil, for misting or brushing

Kosher salt

Tartar sauce, lemon wedges and snipped chives, for serving

═ QUICK & EASY ═

Fish 'n' Chips

ACTIVE TIME 10 min. | **TOTAL TIME** 30 min. | **SERVES** 4

1. Cut the fish into equal-size pieces; fold thinner tail ends in half if needed and secure with a toothpick. Dip the cod into the egg whites, then the chips, pressing to help adhere. Spray or brush with oil.

2. Heat the air fryer to 350°F. Working in 2 batches, place the fish in the basket and air fry until golden brown and opaque throughout, 8 to 10 minutes. Sprinkle with salt.

3. Serve the fish with tartar sauce, lemon wedges and chives.

PER SERVING *About 320 calories, 25 g fat (8 g saturated fat), 39 g protein, 776 mg sodium, 40 g carbohydrates, 7 g fiber*

TIP Crush chips right in the bag for less mess. Make a small hole in the top (so air can escape) and roll over the chips with a rolling pin.

4 6-ounce boneless, skinless
  chicken breasts

4 tablespoons pesto

4 tablespoons goat cheese, crumbled

1½ tablespoons olive oil, divided

Kosher salt and pepper

4 to 6 thin slices prosciutto

¼ cup small basil leaves

12 ounces green beans, trimmed

2 large garlic cloves, thinly sliced

‹ Cheesy-Stuffed Chicken with Green Beans

ACTIVE TIME 20 min. | **TOTAL TIME** 25 min. | **SERVES** 4

1. Insert a knife into the thickest part of each chicken breast and move back and forth to create 2½-inch pocket that is as wide as possible without going through.

2. Using a spoon, divide the pesto and goat cheese among the pockets, rub the chicken with ½ tablespoon oil, then season with salt and pepper.

3. Lay the prosciutto slices on a cutting board and place a few small basil leaves in the center of each. Place chicken on top and wrap the prosciutto around the chicken, then place seam side down in the air fryer basket. Air fry at 375°F, 6 minutes.

4. Toss the green beans and garlic with the remaining tablespoon oil and ¼ teaspoon each salt and pepper. Move the chicken to one side of the air fryer basket and place the green beans on the other side. Continue air frying until the chicken is cooked through and the green beans are just tender and slightly charred. Serve with tomato salad if desired.

PER SERVING *About 380 calories, 19.5 g fat (5 g saturated fat), 43 g protein, 930 mg sodium, 7 g carbohydrates, 2 g fiber*

2 cups grape tomatoes, halved

2 garlic cloves, pressed

4 teaspoons olive oil, divided

Kosher salt and pepper

4 6-ounce boneless, skinless
  chicken breasts

8 ounces fresh mozzarella
  balls, halved

½ cup fresh basil, torn

Chicken Caprese

ACTIVE TIME 10 min. | **TOTAL TIME** 25 min. | **SERVES** 4

1. In a bowl, toss the tomatoes with the garlic, 2 teaspoons oil and pinch each of salt and pepper. Heat the air fryer to 400°F. Place the tomatoes in the basket and air fry until tender and some burst, 3 to 4 minutes. Remove from the basket and transfer to a bowl; set aside.

2. Brush the chicken with the remaining 2 teaspoons oil and sprinkle with ¼ teaspoon each salt and pepper. Air fry at 400°F until cooked through, 5 to 6 minutes. Transfer the cutlets to plates.

3. Fold the mozzarella and basil into the tomatoes and spoon over the chicken.

PER SERVING *About 430 calories, 24 g fat (10 g saturated fat), 43 g protein, 381 mg sodium, 11 g carbohydrates, 4 g fiber*

10 small pieces chicken (3 pounds), breasts halved

1½ cups low-fat buttermilk

3 tablespoons cayenne pepper hot sauce

1 teaspoon garlic powder

Kosher salt and pepper

2 cups all-purpose flour

2 large eggs

Olive oil, for misting or brushing

Hot Honey Sauce (see below), for serving (optional)

Buttermilk Fried Chicken

ACTIVE TIME 25 min. | **TOTAL TIME** 1 hr. plus chilling time | **SERVES** 5

1. Place a 1-gallon resealable plastic bag in a large bowl. Add the chicken.

2. In another bowl, whisk together the buttermilk, hot sauce, garlic powder and 1 teaspoon salt. Pour over the chicken in the bag; seal and refrigerate 3 to 5 hours.

3. Place the flour and 1 teaspoon each salt and pepper in another 1-gallon resealable bag. Shake to combine. In a shallow bowl, beat the eggs with 2 tablespoons water. Remove the chicken from the marinade and discard the marinade. One piece at a time, shake the chicken in the flour bag to coat. Shake off the excess flour and dip in the egg, letting the excess drip off. Return to the flour, shaking to coat again. Shake off the excess, then spray or brush chicken all over with oil.

4. Heat the air fryer to 350°F. Spray or brush the air fryer basket with oil. Working in batches, air fry three or four pieces of chicken at a time, turning once, until cooked through, about 20 minutes. Transfer to a wire rack set over a baking sheet. Keep warm in a 250°F oven if desired. Repeat with the remaining chicken.

5. Serve drizzled with Hot Honey Sauce if desired.

PER SERVING *About 505 calories, 21 g fat (6 g saturated fat), 43 g protein, 638 mg sodium, 34 g carbohydrates, 1 g fiber*

Hot Honey Sauce

Microwave ¼ cup honey on 50 percent power just until runny, 30 seconds. Whisk in 2 tablespoons cayenne pepper hot sauce. Makes about ⅓ cup.

1 small acorn squash, peeled, seeded and sliced

2 teaspoons olive oil

1 teaspoon chopped fresh thyme

Kosher salt and pepper

2 boneless, skinless chicken breasts (about 1 pound)

1 tablespoon grated Parmesan cheese

4 slices prosciutto

◂ Prosciutto-Wrapped Chicken with Roasted Squash

ACTIVE TIME 10 min. | **TOTAL TIME** 50 min. | **SERVES** 2

1. Heat the air fryer to 400°F. Toss the squash with the oil, thyme and ¼ teaspoon salt. Place the squash in the air fryer basket and air fry until tender, 15 minutes, shaking basket once. Transfer to a bowl.

2. Meanwhile, season the chicken with ¼ teaspoon pepper and sprinkle with the Parmesan. Wrap each piece with 2 slices prosciutto. Place in the basket and air fry until cooked through (165°F), 20 minutes.

3. Place the squash on top of the chicken and air fry for 3 minutes or until heated.

PER SERVING *About 425 calories, 14 g fat (4 g saturated fat), 56 g protein, 1,059 mg sodium, 19 g carbohydrates, 6 g fiber*

TIP **Turn this easy dinner into the ultimate leftover lunch by slicing the chicken and squash and layering onto a toasty baguette.**

1 pound large peeled and deveined shrimp

1 tablespoon olive oil, plus more for misting or brushing

1 teaspoon lemon zest

1 teaspoon hot paprika

3 garlic cloves, pressed, divided

Kosher salt and pepper

1 head romaine lettuce

1 head radicchio

¼ cup plain nonfat Greek yogurt

3 tablespoons finely grated Parmesan cheese

3 tablespoons lemon juice

1 teaspoon Dijon mustard

1 cup unseasoned croutons

≡ QUICK & EASY ≡

Garlic Shrimp Caesar Salad

ACTIVE TIME 15 min. | **TOTAL TIME** 25 min. | **SERVES** 4

1. In a large bowl, toss the shrimp with the oil, lemon zest, paprika, two-thirds of the garlic and ⅛ teaspoon salt.

2. Thinly slice the romaine lettuce and radicchio and place in a large serving bowl. In a small bowl, whisk the Greek yogurt, Parmesan, lemon juice, mustard, remaining garlic and ¼ teaspoon each salt and pepper.

3. Heat the air fryer to 400°F. Spray or brush the basket with oil. In 2 batches, air fry the shrimp in single layer until opaque throughout, 3 minutes per batch.

4. Toss the dressing with the lettuce mixture in the serving bowl. Top with the shrimp and croutons.

PER SERVING *About 230 calories, 7 g fat (2 g saturated fat), 26 g protein, 1,170 mg sodium, 16 g carbohydrates, 4 g fiber*

◂ Mediterranean Chicken Bowls

1 pound boneless, skinless chicken breasts, cut into 1½-inch pieces

1 tablespoon olive oil

1 teaspoon dried oregano

1 teaspoon ground sumac

Kosher salt and pepper

1 pint grape or cherry tomatoes

1 medium onion, roughly chopped

1 cup couscous

1 teaspoon grated lemon zest plus 1 tablespoon lemon juice, plus lemon wedges for serving

¼ cup chopped fresh dill, divided

Crumbled feta cheese, for topping

ACTIVE TIME 15 min. | **TOTAL TIME** 30 min. | **SERVES** 4

1. In a large bowl, toss the chicken with the oil, then the oregano, sumac and ½ teaspoon each salt and pepper. Add the tomatoes and onion and toss to combine.

2. Heat the air fryer to 400°F. Arrange the chicken and vegetables in an even layer in the air fryer basket and air fry until the chicken is golden brown and cooked through, 15 to 20 minutes, shaking the basket occasionally.

3. Meanwhile, toss the couscous with the lemon zest and prepare per the package directions. Fluff with a fork and fold in the lemon juice and 2 tablespoons of the dill.

4. Serve the chicken and vegetables over the couscous, spooning any juices collected at bottom of air fryer over the top. Sprinkle with the remaining dill and the feta and serve with lemon wedges if desired.

PER SERVING *About 475 calories, 9.5 g fat (1.5 g saturated fat), 43 g protein, 425 mg sodium, 53 g carbohydrates, 5 g fiber*

TIP Do not chop the onions too small or they may fall through the fry basket.

Ultimate Fried Chicken Sandwich

¾ cup low-fat buttermilk

2 teaspoons garlic powder

Kosher salt and pepper

4 boneless, skinless chicken thighs (about 1 pound)

¾ cup panko breadcrumbs

1 tablespoon canola oil, plus oil for misting or brushing

1 cup all-purpose flour

4 potato rolls

Sliced tomatoes, pickles, romaine leaves and mayonnaise for topping

ACTIVE TIME 15 min. | **TOTAL TIME** 35 min. plus chilling time | **SERVES** 4

1. In a large bowl, combine the buttermilk, garlic powder and ½ teaspoon each salt and pepper. Add the chicken and refrigerate for 1 hour.

2. Place the panko in a resealable plastic bag and crush with a rolling pin. Transfer to a shallow bowl and toss with the oil until evenly coated. Place the flour in another shallow dish.

3. One piece at a time, remove the chicken thighs from the buttermilk, allowing the excess to drip off. Dip in the flour, then in the buttermilk, then in the panko, pressing gently to adhere. Repeat with remaining chicken. Spray or brush both sides with oil.

4. Heat the air fryer to 375°F. Place the chicken in the basket and air fry until golden brown and cooked through, 10 to 12 minutes. Serve the chicken on rolls, topped with tomatoes, pickles, romaine leaves and mayonnaise.

PER SERVING *About 575 calories, 15 g fat (3 g saturated fat), 39 g protein, 622 mg sodium, 67 g carbohydrates, 2 g fiber*

1 pound red potatoes, cut into
   1-inch chunks

2 teaspoons olive oil

Kosher salt and pepper

1 pound lean ground beef (90 percent)

3/4 cup crumbled feta cheese

1/2 small red onion, grated

1/3 cup Italian seasoned breadcrumbs

1/4 cup chopped fresh flat-leaf parsley,
   plus more for topping

1 large egg, lightly beaten

2 teaspoons dried oregano

1/2 cup prepared tzatziki sauce

Lemon slices, for serving

‹ Greek-Style Meatballs

ACTIVE TIME 20 min. | **TOTAL TIME** 50 min. | **SERVES** 4

1. Heat the air fryer to 400°F. In a medium bowl, toss the potatoes with the oil, 1/4 teaspoon salt and 1/8 teaspoon pepper. Air fry the potatoes, shaking the basket occasionally, until browned and cooked through, 14 minutes. Transfer to a plate.

2. Meanwhile, in a large bowl, combine the ground beef, feta, red onion, breadcrumbs, parsley, egg, oregano and 1/4 teaspoon each salt and pepper. Form into 12 meatballs (about 1/4 cup each) and thread onto 6-inch skewers (make sure to soak them in cold water for 15 minutes). Air fry the meatballs, turning once, until cooked through, 10 minutes. Transfer to a plate.

3. Return the potatoes to the basket and air fry until hot, 2 minutes. Serve the potatoes and meatballs with tzatziki and lemon slices and sprinkle with additional parsley if desired.

PER SERVING *About 480 calories, 23 g fat (10 g saturated fat), 34 g protein, 1,165 mg sodium, 35 g carbohydrates, 3 g fiber*

TIP It's important to choose leaner ground beef for this recipe. When we tried making these with meat that had a higher fat percentage, they turned out too brown and crusty.

8 ounces russet or yellow potatoes

1 1/2 teaspoons vegetable oil

Kosher salt and pepper

2 tablespoons mayonnaise

1/4 small shallot, finely chopped

1 teaspoon lemon juice

1/2 teaspoon finely chopped fresh
   tarragon, plus more for topping

2 thin (3/8-inch-thick) boneless top
   sirloin steaks (about 12 ounces)

Fast Steak Frites

ACTIVE TIME 15 min. | **TOTAL TIME** 35 min. | **SERVES** 2

1. Cut the potatoes into 1/4-inch sticks; soak in water for 10 minutes. Drain and pat dry. Toss the potatoes with the oil and 1/4 teaspoon each salt and pepper.

2. Heat the air fryer to 375°F. Place the potatoes in the air fryer basket and air fry for 15 minutes, shaking the basket twice.

3. Meanwhile, combine the mayonnaise, shallot, lemon juice, 1 teaspoon water, tarragon and 1/8 teaspoon pepper.

4. Raise the air fryer temperature to 400°F. Season the steaks with 1/4 teaspoon each salt and pepper. Air fry the steaks to desired doneness, 6 minutes for medium-rare, turning halfway. Transfer the steaks to a cutting board and let rest for 2 minutes. Place the potatoes in the basket and air fry for 2 minutes to warm.

5. Serve the fries with the steak and mayo and sprinkle with chopped tarragon.

PER SERVING *About 490 calories, 27 g fat (7 g saturated fat), 38 g protein, 650 mg sodium, 22 g carbohydrates, 2 g fiber*

2 large eggs

2 teaspoons balsamic vinegar

Kosher salt and pepper

1/3 cup panko breadcrumbs

4 large garlic cloves (2 grated and
2 chopped)

1/4 cup grated Parmesan cheese, plus
more for topping

1/2 cup chopped fresh flat-leaf parsley

8 ounces sweet Italian sausage,
casings removed

8 ounces ground beef

1 pound cherry tomatoes

1 red chile, sliced

1 tablespoon olive oil

6 tablespoons ricotta cheese

4 small hero rolls, split and toasted

Chopped fresh basil, for topping
(optional)

◂ Meatball Subs

ACTIVE TIME 20 min. | **TOTAL TIME** 30 min. | **SERVES** 4

1. In a large bowl, whisk together the eggs, vinegar and 1/2 teaspoon each salt and pepper. Stir in the panko and let sit for 1 minute. Stir in the grated garlic and Parmesan, then the parsley. Add the sausage and ground beef and gently mix to combine. Shape the meat mixture into 20 balls (about 1 1/2 inches each).

2. Heat the air fryer to 400°F. Place the meatballs in a single layer on the air fryer rack (the balls can touch but should not be stacked; cook in batches if necessary) and air fry for 5 minutes.

3. In a bowl, toss the tomatoes, chile and chopped garlic with the oil and 1/4 teaspoon each salt and pepper. Scatter over the meatballs and continue air frying until the meatballs are cooked through, 5 to 6 minutes more.

4. Spread the ricotta on the toasted rolls, then top with meatballs, more Parmesan, tomatoes and basil if desired.

PER SERVING *About 690 calories, 25 g fat (7.5 g saturated fat), 34 g protein, 1,180 mg sodium, 83 g carbohydrates, 7 g fiber*

TIP Make an extra batch to stash in the freezer for last-minute meals.

1/3 cup reduced-sodium soy sauce

1/3 cup apple cider vinegar

2 tablespoons brown sugar

1 teaspoon ground ginger

1/2 teaspoon garlic powder

4 bone-in country-style pork ribs
(about 2 pounds)

3 tablespoons barbecue sauce

2 tablespoons hoisin sauce

Sesame seeds, for topping (optional)

Cabbage slaw, for serving
(see page 153)

Hoisin Barbecue
Country Pork Ribs

ACTIVE TIME 15 min. | **TOTAL TIME** 45 min. plus marinating time | **SERVES** 4

1. In a heavy resealable plastic bag, combine the soy sauce, vinegar, brown sugar, ginger, garlic powder and 1/4 cup water. Add the ribs, shake to combine, push out all the air and seal. Refrigerate for 2 to 8 hours, turning the bag over occasionally.

2. Drain and discard the marinade. In a small bowl, stir together the barbecue sauce and hoisin sauce.

3. Heat the air fryer to 350°F. Place the ribs in the basket, overlapping if needed. Air fry for 30 minutes, turning the ribs every 10 minutes and brushing lightly with hoisin barbecue sauce. Brush with the remaining sauce, sprinkle with sesame seeds if desired and serve with slaw.

PER SERVING *About 510 calories, 38 g fat (14 g saturated fat), 28 g protein, 547 mg sodium, 11 g carbohydrates, 0 g fiber*

1 large red bell pepper, quartered lengthwise, then sliced crosswise

1 large yellow bell pepper, quartered lengthwise, then sliced crosswise

1 large red onion, sliced ¼ inch thick

2 teaspoons grated lime zest plus 2 tablespoons lime juice, plus lime wedges for serving

¼ teaspoon ground cumin

1 tablespoon plus 2 teaspoons canola oil, divided

½ teaspoon granulated garlic, divided

Kosher salt and pepper

12 ounces skirt steak (cut crosswise into 4-inch pieces) or hanger steak (halved)

1 teaspoon ancho chili powder

¼ cup chopped fresh cilantro, plus more for topping

8 6-inch flour tortillas, warmed

Sour cream, for serving

◂ Steak Fajitas

ACTIVE TIME 15 min. | **TOTAL TIME** 35 min. | **SERVES** 4

1. In a large bowl, toss the peppers, onion, lime zest and juice, cumin, 1 tablespoon of the oil, ¼ teaspoon granulated garlic, ½ teaspoon salt and ¼ teaspoon pepper. Heat the air fryer to 400°F. Air fry the peppers and onions for 10 minutes, shaking occasionally.

2. Meanwhile, rub the steak with the remaining 2 teaspoons oil, then season with the ancho chili powder, the remaining ¼ teaspoon granulated garlic and ½ teaspoon each salt and pepper. Push the vegetables to one side of the air fryer and add the steak to the other side. Air fry to desired doneness, 10 minutes for medium-rare, flipping once.

3. Transfer the steak to a cutting board and let rest for at least 5 minutes before slicing. Toss the vegetables with the cilantro. Fill tortillas with steak and peppers, then top with sour cream. Sprinkle with cilantro and serve with lime wedges if desired.

PER SERVING *About 615 calories, 28 g fat (8 g saturated fat), 35 g protein, 1,500 mg sodium, 57 g carbohydrates, 6 g fiber*

1 pound ground turkey

½ cup chopped fresh cilantro

2 garlic cloves, pressed

1 teaspoon chili powder

Kosher salt

Olive oil, for misting or brushing

½ avocado

2 teaspoons lime juice

4 toasted whole-grain sandwich thins

Tomato, cucumber, lettuce, and sprouts, for serving

Turkey Burgers

ACTIVE TIME 15 min. | **TOTAL TIME** 40 min. | **SERVES** 4

1. In a bowl, combine the turkey, cilantro, garlic, chili powder and ¼ teaspoon salt. Form into four patties, making a slight indentation in the center of each. Spray or brush the patties on both sides with oil.

2. Heat the air fryer to 400°F. Air fry in two batches, turning once, until cooked through, 10 to 12 minutes.

3. Mash the avocado with the lime juice. Place the burgers on the sandwich thins; top with avocado and tomato, cucumber, lettuce and sprouts as desired. Serve with sweet potato fries.

PER SERVING *About 265 calories, 6 g fat (1 g saturated fat), 33 g protein, 395 mg sodium, 25 g carbohydrates, 7 g fiber*

TIP Serve with prepared frozen sweet potato fries.

6 ounces rice noodles

½ cup Asian-style sesame dressing

1 large carrot, shaved with a julienne peeler or cut into matchsticks

½ English cucumber, shaved with a julienne peeler or cut into matchsticks

1 scallion, thinly sliced

1 large egg

2 teaspoons grated lime zest plus 2 tablespoons lime juice

1½ tablespoons honey

1 teaspoon fish sauce

Kosher salt

½ cup panko breadcrumbs

1 garlic clove, grated

2 scallions, finely chopped

1 tablespoon grated peeled fresh ginger

1 small jalapeño, seeded and finely chopped

1 pound ground pork

¼ cup chopped fresh cilantro

Gingery Pork Meatballs

ACTIVE TIME 30 min. | **TOTAL TIME** 45 min. | **SERVES** 4

1. Cook the noodles per the package directions. Rinse under cold water to cool, drain well and transfer to a large bowl. Toss with the dressing, carrot, cucumber and scallion; set aside.

2. In a large bowl, whisk together the egg, lime zest and lime juice, honey, fish sauce and ½ teaspoon salt; stir in the panko and let sit for 1 minute. Stir in garlic, scallions, ginger and jalapeño, then add the pork and cilantro and mix to combine. Shape the mixture into tablespoon-size balls.

3. Heat the air fryer to 400°F. Air fry the meatballs in batches, if necessary (balls can touch but should not be stacked), until browned and cooked through, 8 to 12 minutes, shaking basket occasionally. Fold the cilantro into the noodles and serve with the meatballs.

PER SERVING *About 620 calories, 31.5 g fat (8.5 g saturated fat), 26 g protein, 750 mg sodium, 59 g carbohydrates, 2 g fiber*

TIP Don't take out another pot to cook the rice noodles! Place rice noodles in a bowl and cover with bowling water. Let sit until soft and pliable, 8 to 15 minutes (times will differ depending on noodle type and thickness).

Chapter 6

The Instant Pot

::

If you're looking for a one-pot wonder that does it all, the Instant Pot may be just what you're after. This electric multicooker combines the benefits of multiple kitchen appliances in one space-saving kitchen machine. This all-in-one appliance has many functions, including pressure cooking, slow cooking, rice cooking, steaming, warming and sautéing. With a press of a button, the Instant Pot has simplified everyday cooking by reducing cooking times and helping to serve delicious meals even faster.

What's the difference between an Instant Pot, a pressure cooker and a slow cooker?
Even though an Instant Pot can function as a pressure cooker, they're not interchangeable. To help clear the confusion, the Kitchen Appliances Lab experts broke down the differences between these appliance terms:

Pressure cookers offer an easy way to get food on the table fast. Whether it's an electric pressure cooker or stovetop pressure cooker, a pressure cooker drastically reduces cook time (up to 70 percent) by raising the boiling point of water and trapping the steam. Once your food is done cooking, you can either release the pressure manually with the knob or wait for the steam to naturally release. Stovetop models can cook at a higher pressure than electric pressure cookers and therefore get hotter, so an electric cooker may take a bit longer to heat up and cook than its stovetop counterparts (but don't worry, it'll still shave hours off your cook time).

Slow cookers are great for people who want to come home from work to a hot dinner waiting for them. They're called "set it and forget it" appliances for a reason: Just throw ingredients in the slow cooker in the morning, and it'll cook on low heat throughout the day. You can often set them to cook for a certain number of hours and then have it switch to a keep warm setting. You can use the Instant Pot for slow cooking but for more on slow cookers, turn to Chapter 7.

Instant Pot is the most popular multicooker brand, and basically all of the above! It has pressure cooker and slow cooker functions, among others. This chapter features recipes for the pressure cooker function, but any recipe in Chapter 7 can be made in the Instant Pot on the slow cooker function.

Are Instant Pots dangerous?

While pressure cookers of the past might have been dicey safety-wise, you don't need to worry about modern electric pressure cookers in the same way. The appliance is comprised of an outer pot (or base), an inner pot and a lid, all of which have many safety mechanisms built-in such as a sensor that causes steam to release when there's too much pressure in the pot. As an added safety feature, the Instant Pot also features a floating valve, an indicator that pops up when it's unsafe to open the lid while cooking foods. When the floating valve is raised, the lid will automatically lock when it's at a pressure level that could be dangerous to open.

How do you release pressure when cooking is complete?

To release the pressure post-cooking, you can either use the quick release feature, which ejects steam from the pot quickly (typically over 1 to 2 minutes), or a natural release, which lets out steam over time. Your recipe will indicate whether you should use quick or natural release, but as a rule of thumb, natural release is best for stews and other foods that won't overcook, while quick release is recommended for dishes like pasta that are at risk of overcooking.

If you're ready to add an Instant Pot to your kitchen lineup, here are some questions to think about.

How to Choose an Instant Pot

What size do I need?

The Instant Pot comes in different sizes: 3-, 6- and 8-quart. So, which one should you choose? The 6-quart option is the most practical, because it's big enough for a decent-size batch of chicken soup or chili without hogging too much counter space. If you have a larger family or love to meal prep, you might want to consider the 8-quart model.

Are there any accessories that I should buy?

Now for the fun part: dressing up your new multicooker to maximize its use. Here are the Lab's top picks to upgrade your appliance.

Nonstick-Coated Inner Cooking Pot

Instant Pots come with a stainless steel inner cooking pot, but if you're partial to cooking with nonstick pots and pans, you may want to snag a nonstick insert as well. Its ceramic-coated nonstick exterior cleans up beautifully and can go in the dishwasher and the oven (up to 680°F).

Silicone Steam Rack This handy steamer rack features stay-cool arms that can easily (and safely) be lifted out of your Instant Pot after a high-temperature steaming session. Because you can stack up to three on top of one another inside the pot, they're lifesavers when making steaming batches of delicate foods like fish or dumplings.

SPICY SESAME
RICE BOWLS
195

GH
KITCHEN
APPLIANCES
LAB

TOP-TESTED INSTANT POTS

The Kitchen Appliances and Technology Lab evaluates multicookers for how well they pressure cook and slow cook a beef stew and their ability to evenly brown meat and make rice. It also tested how quickly they came up to pressure and released pressure both quickly and naturally. Plus, the culinary pros check each multicooker ease of use, including how intuitive and easy-to-read the controls are, the variety of settings offered, how easy it is to clean the cooking insert and the clarity of the owner's manual.

BEST OVERALL
Instant Pot Duo

The Duo offers all of the standard Instant Pot features with an extra setting for making homemade yogurt. It comes in 3-, 6- and 8-quart options and claims to replace seven common kitchen appliances. The inner pot is made of stainless steel, and it boasts a three-ply bottom for even heat distribution, "delay start" and "keep warm" functions and low- and high-pressure options that allow you to have more control over the cooking temperature. Additional user-friendly features include a large handle on the top making opening and closing quick and easy, extra slots on both side handles to prop up the lid when it's not in use and a detachable cord for easy storage.

**SCAN FOR MORE
INSTANT POT
LAB REVIEWS**

Cooking Tips for Best Results

1. **Cut food into smaller pieces.** A general rule of cooking, this technique does not change when working with an Instant Pot. Since pressure can often speed up the cooking process, uniform pieces of food are arguably even more important to consider.

2. **Add liquid.** Always have at least ½ cup of liquid in the pot. Anything less and you'll likely run into the burn error—liquid is needed to create steam which turns into pressure in a closed environment. As recipes cook, the liquid cooks off and without it, pressure can't be created.

3. **Consider the time it takes to come to pressure.** Your Instant Pot takes time to come to pressure first before the actual cooking process begins. Expect meals that are mostly liquid (like a soup) to take a while to come to pressure, while those with less liquid will start cooking more quickly. When cooking some foods, you can set the time to zero: the ingredient will cook in the time it takes the Instant Pot to come to pressure.

4. **Allow more time for frozen foods.** The Instant Pot's pressure cooker function is great in a pinch or on nights you forgot to defrost chicken for dinner. That said, cooking any food from frozen will increase the amount of time it takes for your cooker to pressurize.

5. **Use tongs if using the quick release.** Hot steam can burn bare fingers when turning the release valve. To be safe, use tongs or another cooking utensil to flip the release valve. And make sure to strategically place your appliance before cooking: heat and steam can damage kitchen cabinets with repeated exposure.

6. **Use the sauté function.** After pressure cooking, use sauté to thicken sauces or gravies. Because there's no evaporation when the lid is sealed, braised recipes can end up with thinner liquids than you may want. Flip on the sauté function at the end to cook down sauces before serving.

7. **The handle is a built-in lid holder.** Extra slots on the side handles prop up the lid when it's not in use.

8. **Replace the ring.** Every 18 to 24 months, replace the silicone sealing ring. It will stretch over time with normal use, and it can also discolor. If you like cooking sweet and savory dishes in the appliance, you can keep two sealing rings on hand to switch between.

9. **The entire lid is dishwasher-safe.** The manual states that the lid can be placed on the top rack of a dishwasher. Just make sure to remove the sealing ring and anti-block shield on the bottom side of the lid.

10. **Remember food safety.** The Instant Pot's automatic keep warm setting can help keep food out of the "danger zone" (the temperature range in which bacteria rapidly multiply in food, which spans between 40°F and 140°F according to the U.S. Food and Drug Administration).

SO, WHAT IS PHO?

Pho (pronounced "fuh," as in "duh") is a traditional Vietnamese soup made of bone broth, rice noodles, bean sprouts, herbs, and meat. Most commonly, it's made with chicken or beef, but there are vegetarian and even vegan versions, too. The warm and comforting soup is a staple street food in Vietnam, but lately it has taken the culinary world by storm, so now you can find it anywhere.

4 star anise pods

1 small cinnamon stick, smashed

1 teaspoon coriander seeds, crushed

½ teaspoon black peppercorns

4 whole cloves

1 2-inch piece fresh ginger, peeled, quartered and then smashed

½ red onion, coarsely chopped

½ Fuji apple

1½ pounds bone-in chicken thighs, skin removed

2 tablespoons fish sauce, divided

3 ounces instant rice noodles

Bean sprouts, sliced red chile, chopped red onion, chopped fresh mint or cilantro and lime wedges, for serving (optional)

‹ Pho with Chicken

ACTIVE TIME 20 min. | **TOTAL TIME** 1 hr. | **SERVES** 4

1. Press Sauté on the Instant Pot and add the star anise, cinnamon, coriander, peppercorns and cloves and sauté until fragrant, 3 to 4 minutes.

2. Add the ginger and onion and cook, stirring occasionally, for 4 minutes. Add the apple, chicken, 5 cups water and 1 tablespoon of the fish sauce. Cover and lock the lid, and cook on high pressure 22 minutes. Allow to natural release for 10 minutes, then release any remaining pressure.

3. Transfer the chicken to a plate. Strain the broth, discarding the remaining solids. Return the broth to the pot, add the noodles and let sit until tender, 3 to 4 minutes.

4. Meanwhile, shred the chicken, discarding the bones. Return the chicken to the pot and stir in the remaining tablespoon fish sauce. Serve with toppings such as bean sprouts, red chile, red onion, mint or cilantro and lime wedges.

PER SERVING *About 235 calories, 5 g fat (1.5 g saturated fat), 23 g protein, 730 mg sodium, 22 g carbohydrates, 0 g fiber*

1 3- to 3½-pound chicken, including neck (discard giblets), skin removed

2 large carrots, halved

2 stalks celery, halved

1 onion, quartered

1 garlic clove, smashed

1 bay leaf

4 flat-leaf parsley sprigs

Kosher salt

1½ cups egg noodles

Chopped fresh dill and celery leaves, for topping (optional)

≡ QUICK & EASY ≡
Chicken Soup

ACTIVE TIME 10 min. | **TOTAL TIME** 30 min. | **SERVES** 6

1. Add the chicken, carrots, celery, onion, garlic, bay leaf, parsley, ¾ teaspoon salt and 6 cups water. Lock the lid and cook on high pressure for 15 minutes. Use the quick release method and then open the lid. Transfer the chicken to a bowl and the carrots and celery to a cutting board; let cool.

2. Strain the broth through a fine-mesh sieve, discarding any remaining solids; transfer back to the pot. Press Sauté on the Instant Pot and bring the broth to a simmer. Add the noodles and cook until tender, 5 to 6 minutes.

3. Meanwhile, cut the carrots and celery into small chunks and shred the chicken into large pieces, discarding the skin and bones. Stir the vegetables and chicken into the broth. Serve the soup sprinkled with dill and celery leaves if desired.

PER SERVING *About 305 calories, 16 g fat (4.5 g saturated fat), 28 g protein, 345 mg sodium, 11 g carbohydrates, 2 g fiber*

1 pound beef chuck, well trimmed and cut into 2-inch pieces

1 tablespoon all-purpose flour

1 tablespoon olive oil

1 large onion, chopped

4 garlic cloves, smashed

8 thyme sprigs, plus leaves for serving

Kosher salt and pepper

1 12-ounce bottle beer

½ medium butternut squash (1 pound), peeled, seeded and cut into 2-inch pieces

3 medium carrots, sliced

3 cups low-sodium beef broth

1 cup pearled barley

‹ Beef & Barley Stew

ACTIVE TIME 15 min. | **TOTAL TIME** 55 min. | **SERVES** 4

1. In a medium bowl, toss the beef with the flour. Press Sauté on the Instant Pot and heat the oil. Add the beef and cook until browned on all sides, 5 to 6 minutes. Transfer the beef to a plate.

2. Add the onion, garlic, thyme sprigs and ½ teaspoon each salt and pepper to the pot and cook, stirring occasionally, until tender, 5 to 6 minutes. Stir in the beer.

3. Return the beef to the pot along with squash, carrots, beef broth and barley. Lock the lid and cook on high pressure for 16 minutes. Use the quick release method and then open the lid. Serve sprinkled with additional thyme if desired.

PER SERVING *About 485 calories, 9 g fat (2 g saturated fat), 35 g protein, 490 mg sodium, 67 g carbohydrates, 13 g fiber*

1 tablespoon unsalted butter

1 tablespoon olive oil

1 medium onion, finely chopped

2 garlic cloves, finely chopped

1½ cups Arborio rice

Kosher salt

½ cup dry white wine

3½ cups low-sodium chicken broth

½ cup grated Parmesan cheese, plus more for topping

Cracked black pepper (optional)

Risotto with Parmesan

ACTIVE TIME 15 min. | **TOTAL TIME** 35 min. | **SERVES** 4

1. Press Sauté on the Instant Pot and heat butter and oil. Add onions and cook, stirring occassionally, until tender, 6 minutes. Stir in the garlic and cook for 2 minutes.

2. Stir in the rice and 1 teaspoon salt and cook, stirring occasionally, until golden brown and toasted, 4 to 6 minutes. Add the wine and cook until absorbed, about 1 minute. Stir in the broth.

3. Cover, lock the lid and cook on high pressure for 5 minutes. Use the quick release method and then open the lid. Stir the risotto until the liquid has been absorbed, 2 to 3 minutes. Stir in the Parmesan. Serve with additional Parmesan and cracked pepper if desired.

PER SERVING *About 406 calories, 11 g fat (4 g saturated fat), 14 g protein, 727 mg sodium, 65 g carbohydrates, 4 g fiber*

TIP Switch it up! Risotto is a great base for many other delicious flavor combos. Try switching it up with spinach and scallions, peas and lemon zest or pesto and egg.

4 pounds bone-in beef short ribs

1 tablespoon olive oil

Kosher salt and pepper

2 stalks celery, chopped

1 medium carrot, chopped

2 garlic cloves, pressed

2 tablespoons tomato paste

3 cups dry red wine

1 pound small shallots (about 8), halved or quartered if large, root end left intact

1½ teaspoons Worcestershire sauce

2 thyme sprigs

2 bay leaves

1 rosemary sprig

1 cup low-sodium chicken broth or water

Red Wine–Braised Short Ribs with Shallots

ACTIVE TIME 1 hr. | **TOTAL TIME** 2 hr. 30 min. | **SERVES** 6

1. Press Sauté on the Instant Pot and heat oil. Pat the short ribs dry and season with ½ teaspoon each salt and pepper, then working in batches, cook the short ribs until browned on all sides, 10 to 12 minutes per batch. Transfer to a bowl.

2. Add the celery, carrot and garlic to the pot and cook, stirring occasionally, until tender, 3 to 4 minutes. Push the vegetables to the outside of the pot and add the tomato paste to the center. Cook, without stirring, until the bottom of the pot is browned, about 1 minute.

3. Add the wine and simmer until reduced by half, 18 to 20 minutes. Add the shallots, Worcestershire sauce, thyme, bay leaves, rosemary and broth. Return the ribs and any juices to the pot. Close and lock the lid.

4. Cook on high pressure for 40 minutes. Allow to natural release for 15 minutes, then release any remaining pressure.

5. Transfer the short ribs (and any loose bones) and the shallots to a platter. Discard the herb sprigs and bay leaves. Skim off any excess fat; then, using an immersion blender (or a standard blender), puree the sauce until smooth, adding a pinch of salt if necessary. Serve the sauce over the short ribs.

PER SERVING *About 785 calories, 63 g fat (18 g saturated fat), 34.5 g protein, 295 mg sodium, 18 g carbohydrates, 3 g fiber*

2 slices smoked bacon, diced

1 small onion, thinly sliced

1 red bell pepper, thinly sliced

2 large garlic cloves, thinly sliced

Pinch red pepper flakes

Kosher salt and ground black pepper

1 14½-ounce can diced tomatoes

¼ cup old-fashioned or
stone-ground grits

⅔ cup whole milk

2 cups corn kernels (from 2 large ears
or frozen)

1 pound peeled and deveined
large shrimp

½ tablespoon lemon juice

½ cup sliced fresh basil, divided

Shrimp & Grits

ACTIVE TIME 25 min. | **TOTAL TIME** 55 min. | **SERVES** 4

1. Press Sauté on the Instant Pot and adjust to medium. Cook the bacon, stirring occasionally until crisp, 8 minutes. With a slotted spoon, transfer to a paper towel–lined plate.

2. Add the onion, bell pepper, garlic, red pepper flakes and ¼ teaspoon each salt and black pepper and cook, stirring occasionally, for 5 minutes. (If the mixture starts to scorch, turn sauté function to low.) Stir in the tomatoes with juice and press Cancel. Place the steam rack on top of the tomato mixture.

3. In a 2-quart (7-inch) baking dish that fits inside the Instant Pot, stir together the grits, milk, ⅔ cup water and ¼ teaspoon salt. Place the dish on top of the rack. Lock the lid and cook on high pressure for 10 minutes. Let pressure release naturally.

4. Meanwhile, place the corn in a large bowl. Cover with boiling water and let sit for 5 minutes.

5. Remove the grits and steam rack from the Instant Pot. Stir the shrimp and lemon juice into the tomato mixture. Cook using the sauté function, stirring occasionally, until the shrimp are opaque throughout, 3 to 5 minutes. Stir in half the basil.

6. Drain the corn and stir it into the grits, adding more milk to adjust consistency if desired. Spoon the grits into bowls. Top with the shrimp mixture and sprinkle with bacon and the remaining basil.

PER SERVING *About 305 calories, 9 g fat (3 g saturated fat), 23 g protein, 1,240 mg sodium, 34 g carbohydrates, 4 g fiber*

TIP To easily peel and devein shrimp, grab a pair of kitchen shears! Using shears, follow the curve of the shrimp's back to cut through the shell and just a bit of the flesh to expose the vein. Use the tip of the scissors or a paring knife to remove the vein. Then remove the shell if desired.

13/4 pounds pork shoulder, trimmed and cut into 4 pieces

Kosher salt and pepper

1 tablespoon olive oil

1 small ripe pineapple

1/2 small red onion, thinly sliced

1/4 cup lime juice

1/4 medium red cabbage (about 8 ounces)

1 12-count package slider rolls (we used King's Hawaiian)

1 cup chopped fresh cilantro

Hawaiian Pork Pull-Apart Rolls

ACTIVE TIME 35 min. | **TOTAL TIME** 1 hr. 20 min. | **SERVES** 6

1. Season the pork with 1 teaspoon each salt and pepper. Press Sauté on the Instant Pot, add the oil and cook the pork, turning occasionally, until browned on all sides, about 7 minutes. Press Cancel.

2. Meanwhile, peel and core the pineapple. Cut half of it into 1-inch pieces and add to the Instant Pot. Cover and lock the lid. Cook on high pressure for 35 minutes. Let release naturally for 10 minutes, then manually release any remaining pressure.

3. Meanwhile, in a large bowl, toss the onion, lime juice and 1/4 teaspoon each salt and pepper. Core the cabbage, then finely shred it and toss with the onion. Thinly slice the remaining pineapple into rounds, then cut crosswise into matchsticks and reserve.

4. Transfer the pork and cooked pineapple to a bowl and shred the pork into pieces. Add 1/2 cup cooking liquid and toss to coat.

5. Cut the slider rolls horizontally (do not break apart) and place the bottom halves on a platter. Toss the pineapple matchsticks with the cabbage mixture, then fold in the cilantro. Spoon the pork mixture on the rolls, then top with the slaw. Sandwich with the top halves.

PER SERVING *About 445 calories, 18 g fat (6.5 g saturated fat), 27 g protein, 525 mg sodium, 44 g carbohydrates, 3 g fiber*

4 ounces pancetta, chopped

2 teaspoons extra virgin olive oil

3 pounds assorted bone-in,
skin-on chicken pieces

1/2 teaspoon dried thyme

Kosher salt and pepper

1 medium leek, thinly sliced

11/2 cups dry white wine

1 pound golden potatoes, cut
into 1-inch chunks

12 ounces cremini mushrooms,
quartered

Chopped fresh flat-leaf parsley,
for topping

‹ Quicker Coq au Vin Blanc

ACTIVE TIME 10 min. | **TOTAL TIME** 35 min. | **SERVES** 4

1. Press Sauté on the Instant Pot, adjust to medium and cook the pancetta in the oil for 5 to 7 minutes or until the fat has rendered. Transfer the pancetta to a plate.

2. Meanwhile, pat the chicken dry with paper towels; season all over with thyme and 1/2 teaspoon each salt and pepper. In batches, add the chicken, skin side down, to the pot; cook for 6 minutes or until browned on two sides, turning once halfway through. Transfer the chicken to a large plate.

3. To the pot, add the leek and 1/4 teaspoon salt; cook for 3 minutes, stirring. Add the wine. Bring to a boil on high. Reduce the heat; simmer for 5 minutes. Add the potatoes and mushrooms, then return the chicken to the pot. Cover, lock the lid, and cook on high pressure for 8 minutes.

4. Use the quick release method to release the pressure, then open the lid. Serve the chicken and vegetables with some of the cooking liquid. Sprinkle with the parsley.

PER SERVING *About 725 calories, 43 g fat (13 g saturated fat), 52 g protein, 785 mg sodium, 29 g carbohydrates, 2 g fiber*

4 lamb shanks (about 4 pounds total)

Kosher salt and pepper

2 tablespoons all-purpose flour

2 tablespoons olive oil

1 medium onion, chopped

1 tablespoon grated peeled
fresh ginger

2 garlic cloves, pressed

1 141/2-ounce can diced tomatoes

3 carrots, cut into 11/2-inch chunks

1/2 cup dried apricots

1/2 cup raisins

1/2 cup orange juice

1/4 cup honey

Apricot-Braised Lamb Shanks

ACTIVE TIME 15 min. | **TOTAL TIME** 1 hr. | **SERVES** 4

1. Season the lamb shanks with 1/2 teaspoon salt and 1/8 teaspoon pepper and dredge in the flour.

2. Press Sauté on the Instant Pot and heat the oil. Add the shanks, two at a time, and cook for 5 minutes per side or until browned. Transfer to a plate. Add the onion to the pot and cook for 3 minutes or until softened, stirring occasionally. Stir in the ginger and garlic and cook for 1 minute. Press Cancel.

3. Return the shanks to the pot and add the tomatoes and juice, carrots, apricots and raisins. In a measuring cup, stir together the orange juice, honey, 1/2 teaspoon salt and 1/8 teaspoon pepper. Pour the juice over the shanks. Cover, lock the lid and cook on high pressure for 35 minutes. Once the cooking is complete, allow the pressure to release naturally.

4. Serve the shanks with the sauce.

PER SERVING *About 755 calories, 36 g fat (14 g saturated fat), 45 g protein, 1,008 mg sodium, 63 g carbohydrates, 5 g fiber*

2 tablespoons olive oil

1 small onion, chopped

5 ounces cremini mushrooms, sliced

1/2 medium bunch kale, stems discarded, leaves chopped (about 5 packed cups)

2 teaspoons chopped fresh thyme

Kosher salt and pepper

3 large eggs

1 3/4 cups whole milk

1 1/2 teaspoons Dijon mustard

1/4 teaspoon grated nutmeg

Pinch cayenne

2 1-inch-thick slices sourdough bread, cut into cubes (about 2 cups)

1/2 cup coarsely shredded Gruyére cheese

Nonstick cooking spray

1/4 cup grated Parmesan cheese

Savory Bread Pudding

ACTIVE TIME 40 min. | **TOTAL TIME** 1 hr. 15 min. | **SERVES** 6

1. Press Sauté on the Instant Pot, adjust to medium, and heat the oil. Add the onion and mushrooms and cook, stirring occasionally, until golden brown, 8 to 10 minutes. Stir in the kale, thyme and 1/4 teaspoon salt and cook until the kale is wilted and the liquid has evaporated, 3 to 5 minutes. Press Cancel.

2. In a large bowl, whisk together the eggs, milk, mustard, nutmeg, cayenne and 1/4 teaspoon each salt and pepper. Add the bread and toss to coat, then fold in the kale and mushrooms and the Gruyére.

3. Lightly coat six 8-ounce ramekins with cooking spray. Divide the bread mixture among the ramekins, pouring any remaining custard mixture on top, then cover each with foil.

4. Pour 1 cup water into the Instant Pot (no need to rinse) and place a steam rack in the pot. Arrange three ramekins on the rack, then stagger the remaining three ramekins on top to create two layers. Lock the lid and cook on high pressure for 8 minutes. Allow to naturally release for 10 minutes, then release any remaining pressure. Use tongs to transfer the ramekins to a rimmed baking sheet, then carefully remove the foil.

5. Arrange an oven rack in the top third of the oven and heat the broiler. Sprinkle Parmesan on top of each pudding and broil until lightly browned, 3 minutes. Let cool 5 minutes; then, if desired, run a small offset spatula around the rim of each ramekin. Invert to slip out pudding, then set upright on a plate. Repeat with remaining ramekins. Serve warm, with salad if desired.

PER SERVING *About 260 calories, 15 g fat (5.5 g saturated fat), 14 g protein, 505 mg sodium, 18 g carbohydrates, 2 g fiber*

TIP Serve with a simple salad of mixed greens tossed with a red wine vinaigrette dressing.

1 pound ground pork

¼ cup panko breadcrumbs

1 large egg

4 scallions, white and green parts separated and finely chopped

½ cup finely chopped fresh cilantro

4 teaspoons finely grated peeled fresh ginger, divided

2 large garlic cloves, finely grated, divided

Kosher salt and pepper

8 ounces linguine noodles, broken in half

2 tablespoons sesame oil, divided

3 tablespoons creamy peanut butter

1½ tablespoons reduced-sodium soy sauce

1 tablespoon lime juice

1 teaspoon light brown sugar

Thinly sliced red chile, sesame seeds and lime wedges, for serving

Sesame-Peanut Noodles & Meatballs

ACTIVE TIME 35 min. | **TOTAL TIME** 40 min. | **SERVES** 4

1. In a large bowl, combine the pork, panko, egg, scallion whites, cilantro, half of the ginger, two-thirds of the garlic and ¼ teaspoon each salt and pepper. Form the mixture into 1½-inch balls (you should have about 16).

2. In the pot of the Instant Pot, stir together the noodles and 1 tablespoon of the sesame oil to coat. Place the meatballs on top of the noodles, and add 1¾ cups water and ¼ teaspoon salt. Lock the lid and cook on high pressure for 6 minutes. Use the quick release method to release the pressure, then open the lid. Press Cancel.

3. Meanwhile, in a medium bowl, whisk together the peanut butter, soy sauce, lime juice, brown sugar and the remaining sesame oil, ginger and garlic.

4. Stir the peanut sauce into the noodles and meatballs in the pot and cover with the lid. Let sit for 5 minutes, then transfer to serving plates.

5. Top with the scallion greens, red chile and sesame seeds and serve with lime wedges for squeezing.

PER SERVING *About 535 calories, 20 g fat (4.5 g saturated fat), 38 g protein, 735 mg sodium, 53 g carbohydrates, 3 g fiber*

2 medium shallots, thinly sliced

1 tablespoon finely chopped peeled
   fresh ginger

1 tablespoon vegetable oil

1 teaspoon ground coriander

½ teaspoon ground cardamom

1 small butternut squash,
   peeled, seeded, and cut
   into 1½-inch chunks

1 pound green lentils, rinsed and
   picked over

6 cups chicken or vegetable broth

Kosher salt and pepper

5 cups packed baby spinach

1 tablespoon cider vinegar

◂ Winter Squash & Lentil Stew

ACTIVE TIME 15 min. | **TOTAL TIME** 35 min. | **SERVES** 6

1. Press Sauté on the Instant Pot, adjust to medium and cook the shallots and ginger in the oil, stirring, for 5 minutes or until the shallots are golden. Add coriander and cardamom; cook for 1 minute, stirring. Add the squash, lentils, broth and ¼ teaspoon salt.

2. Cover, lock the lid, and cook on high pressure for 12 minutes. Use the quick release method to release the pressure, then open the lid.

3. Stir in the spinach, vinegar and ½ teaspoon each salt and pepper.

PER SERVING *About 325 calories, 4 g fat (.61 g saturated fat), 19 g protein, 705 mg sodium, 57 g carbohydrates, 15 g fiber*

⅓ cup gochujang (Korean hot
   pepper paste)

2 tablespoons sesame oil

1 tablespoon reduced-sodium
   soy sauce

1 tablespoon sugar

3 garlic cloves, pressed

1 pound beef top round, cut
   against the grain into very
   thin 2-inch-long slices

Kosher salt

12 ounces shiitake mushrooms,
   stemmed and sliced

1 seedless (English) cucumber,
   thinly sliced

¼ cup rice vinegar

5 ounces baby spinach

6 cups cooked white rice, hot

Chopped scallions, sliced carrots,
   kimchi and sesame seeds,
   for topping

Spicy Sesame Rice Bowls

ACTIVE TIME 25 min. | **TOTAL TIME** 35 min. | **SERVES** 6

1. In a large bowl, whisk the gochujang, sesame oil, soy sauce, sugar, garlic and ¼ cup water until smooth; set aside ½ cup of sauce. To the bowl with the remaining sauce, add the beef and a pinch of salt, tossing to coat. Let stand at least 10 minutes or refrigerate up to overnight.

2. Add the beef to the Instant Pot along with the mushrooms. Cover, lock the lid, cook on high pressure for 10 minutes.

3. While the beef cooks, toss the cucumber with the vinegar and ¼ teaspoon salt; set aside.

4. Use the quick release method to release the pressure, then open the lid. Divide the spinach among 6 serving bowls; top each with 1 cup cooked rice. Drain the cucumbers. Top the rice with beef and mushrooms, cucumber, scallions, carrots, kimchi and sesame seeds; drizzle with the reserved sauce.

PER SERVING *About 450 calories, 10 g fat (2 g saturated fat), 26 g protein, 710 mg sodium, 65 g carbohydrates, 5 g fiber*

2 tablespoons canola oil, divided

1 red onion, sliced ¼ inch thick

1 large red bell pepper, quartered
lengthwise, then sliced crosswise

Kosher salt and pepper

1 2-pound beef chuck roast, well
trimmed and cut into 3-inch pieces

1 14½-ounce can coconut milk,
well shaken

3 tablespoons Thai red curry paste

Cooked rice, lime wedges, fresh
cilantro and sliced red chile,
for serving

◂ Beef Curry

ACTIVE TIME 15 min. | **TOTAL TIME** 60 min. | **SERVES** 6

1. Press Sauté on the Instant Pot and heat 1 tablespoon oil. Add the onion and bell pepper, season with ¼ teaspoon each salt and pepper and sauté until just tender, 5 minutes; transfer to a bowl.

2. Add the remaining tablespoon oil, season the beef with ¼ teaspoon each salt and pepper and cook until browned on all sides, about 5 minutes.

3. Whisk together coconut milk and curry paste, add to the pot, and scrape up any brown bits. Cover, lock the lid and cook on high pressure for 35 minutes. Allow to natural release for 10 minutes, then release any remaining pressure.

4. Using 2 forks, break up the meat into pieces, then toss with the onion and bell pepper. Serve over rice along with lime wedges and topped with cilantro and red chile if desired.

PER SERVING *About 400 calories, 26 g fat (15.5 g saturated fat), 35 g protein, 480 mg sodium, 7 g carbohydrates, 1 g fiber*

1 tablespoon olive oil

1 large onion, chopped

3 garlic cloves, finely chopped

1½ tablespoons chili powder

¼ teaspoon cayenne

2 teaspoons ground cumin, divided

4 cups low-sodium chicken broth

1 pound dried black beans, picked over
(2½ cups)

1 large red bell pepper, chopped

2 teaspoons kosher salt

⅓ cup coarsely chopped fresh
cilantro, plus more for topping

Yogurt, chopped red onion and lime
wedges, for serving

Spicy Black Bean Soup

ACTIVE TIME 10 min. | **TOTAL TIME** 55 min. | **SERVES** 6

1. Press Sauté on the Instant Pot and heat the oil for 1 to 2 minutes. Add the onion and cook, uncovered, until softened, about 3 minutes. Stir in the garlic, chili powder, cayenne and 1½ teaspoons of the cumin and cook 30 seconds, stirring.

2. Add the broth, beans, bell pepper and 4 cups water to the pot. Cover, lock the lid and cook on high pressure for 30 minutes. Use the quick release. Stir in the salt, cilantro and the remaining ½ teaspoon cumin.

3. To serve, top the soup with dollops of yogurt, red onion and cilantro. Serve with lime wedges.

PER SERVING *About 310 calories, 4 g fat (1 g saturated fat), 17 g protein, 982 mg sodium, 54 g carbohydrates, 14 g fiber*

TIP If you like your soup smooth, you can puree it after cooking using an immersion blender.

1 tablespoon vegetable oil

1 medium onion, finely chopped

1 tablespoon grated peeled
    fresh ginger

3 garlic cloves, pressed

1 tablespoon curry powder

1 teaspoon paprika

1½ pounds boneless, skinless chicken
    thighs, cut into 1½-inch chunks

1 cup canned crushed tomatoes

½ cup Chicken Broth (see page 25)

2 teaspoons sugar

Kosher salt

½ cup half-and-half

1½ teaspoons cornstarch

¼ cup chopped fresh cilantro

Cooked white rice, for serving

◄ No-Time Tikka Masala

ACTIVE TIME 15 min. | **TOTAL TIME** 35 min. | **SERVES** 4

1. Press Sauté on the Instant Pot and heat the oil. Add the onion and cook, stirring occasionally, for 4 minutes or until golden. Add the ginger and garlic; cook for 1 minute, stirring. Add the curry powder and paprika; cook for 30 seconds, stirring. Stir in the chicken, tomatoes, broth, sugar and ¾ teaspoon salt. Press Cancel.

2. Cover, lock the lid, and cook on high pressure for 12 minutes. Use the quick release method to release the pressure, then open the lid.

3. In a measuring cup, mix the half-and-half and cornstarch. Set the pot to sauté and bring the chicken to a simmer. Stir in the half-and-half mixture. Simmer for 2 minutes or until thickened, stirring occasionally. Stir in the cilantro. Serve with rice.

PER SERVING *(WITHOUT RICE) About 335 calories, 14 g fat (4 g saturated fat), 37 g protein, 738 mg sodium, 14 g carbohydrates, 3 g fiber*

TIP **Keep this recipe quick and easy by using precooked rice.**

1 pound dried white kidney beans
    (cannellini) or Great Northern beans

2 onions, sliced in half-rounds

3 tablespoons olive oil, plus more
    for topping

3 slices bacon

4 large garlic cloves, smashed

1 bay leaf

2 sage sprigs, plus 2 teaspoons
    thinly sliced fresh sage

Kosher salt and pepper

Tuscan White Beans with Sage

ACTIVE TIME 15 min. | **TOTAL TIME** 25 min. plus soaking time | **SERVES** 8

1. Place the beans in a large bowl. Add cold water to cover by 2 inches. Let stand overnight. Drain and rinse well.

2. Press Sauté on the Instant Pot and cook the onion in the oil for 4 minutes or until softening. Press Cancel.

3. Add the bacon, garlic, bay leaf, sage sprigs, drained beans and 6 cups water. Cover, lock the lid and cook on high pressure for 7 minutes. Use the quick release method to release the pressure, then open the lid.

4. Drain the beans, reserving 1 cup of the cooking liquid. Discard the bacon, sage sprigs and bay leaf. Stir in 2 teaspoons salt, ¼ teaspoon pepper, the sliced sage and ½ to 1 cup of the cooking liquid to desired consistency. (Note: You can use the leftover bean liquid as a base for soups or stews.) Serve hot, warm or at room temperature. Drizzle with additional olive oil if desired.

PER SERVING *About 263 calories, 7 g fat (1 g saturated fat), 14 g protein, 617 mg sodium, 37 g carbohydrates, 20 g fiber*

1 3- to 3½-pound boneless beef chuck roast

Kosher salt and pepper

1 tablespoon vegetable oil

1 stalk celery, chopped

¾ cup dry red wine

1 14½-ounce can diced tomatoes

4 garlic cloves, smashed

½ teaspoon dried thyme

1 bay leaf

1 pound carrots, cut into 2-inch chunks

1 14-ounce package frozen pearl onions

1 tablespoon cornstarch dissolved in 2 tablespoons water

Pot Roast with Red Wine Sauce

ACTIVE TIME 25 min. | **TOTAL TIME** 2 hr. 30 min. | **SERVES** 8

1. Pat the beef dry with paper towels; season on all sides with ¼ teaspoon each salt and pepper. Press Sauté on the Instant Pot and cook the beef in the oil for 6 minutes, until browned, turning once. Transfer to a plate. Add the celery and wine to the pot and cook for 2 minutes. Stir in the tomatoes and juice, garlic, thyme and bay leaf. Press Cancel.

2. Place the beef on top and press into the sauce. Cover, lock the lid, and cook on high pressure for 1 hour 15 minutes. Once the cooking is complete, allow the pressure to release naturally. Transfer the beef to a cutting board and cover with foil. Discard the bay leaf.

3. Skim off any excess fat from the surface of the sauce. Choose sauté function and adjust the heat to More. Cook for 18 minutes or until reduced by about half (you should have about 2½ cups). Press Cancel.

4. Add the carrots and onions. Cover, lock the lid and cook on high pressure for 4 minutes. Use the quick release method to release the pressure, then open the lid. Using the sauté function, keep at a simmer. Gradually stir in the cornstarch mixture and cook for 1 minute. Season with salt and pepper to taste.

5. Slice the meat across the grain and serve with the vegetables and sauce.

PER SERVING *About 525 calories, 30 g fat (11 g saturated fat), 45 g protein, 318 mg sodium, 15 g carbohydrates, 3 g fiber*

1 3-pound boneless beef
   chuck roast, trimmed

2 tablespoons chili powder

1 10-ounce can diced tomatoes
   with green chiles

1 4-ounce can diced green
   chiles, drained

1/2 cup light mayonnaise

3 scallions, finely chopped

2 tablespoons lime juice

Sandwich rolls and lettuce,
   for serving

Tex-Mex Beef Sammies

ACTIVE TIME 10 min. | **TOTAL TIME** 1 hr. 25 min. | **SERVES** 12

1. Rub the beef with the chili powder. Pour the tomatoes and juice into the Instant Pot. Add the beef and top with the green chiles. Cover, lock the lid and cook on high pressure for 1 hour 15 minutes. Use the quick release method to release the pressure.

2. In a small bowl, combine the mayonnaise, scallions and lime juice. Transfer the beef to a cutting board and slice or shred it, discarding any fat. Serve the shredded beef on sandwich rolls with lettuce and the lime mayonnaise.

PER SERVING *About 420 calories, 21 g fat (8 g saturated fat), 22 g protein, 527 mg sodium, 30 g carbohydrates, 2 g fiber*

6 medium bone-in chicken thighs
   (1½ pounds), skin and fat removed

Kosher salt and pepper

1 tablespoon vegetable oil

1 medium onion, finely chopped

1 red bell pepper, coarsely chopped

1 cup long-grain white rice

2 garlic cloves, finely chopped

1/2 teaspoon dried oregano, crumbled

1/4 teaspoon cayenne

1½ cups low-sodium chicken broth

1 cup frozen peas, thawed

1/4 cup pimiento-stuffed
   olives, chopped

1/4 cup chopped fresh cilantro

Lemon wedges, for serving

Arroz con Pollo

ACTIVE TIME 15 min. | **TOTAL TIME** 50 min. plus standing | **SERVES** 4

1. Season the chicken with ½ teaspoon salt and ¼ teaspoon pepper.

2. Press Sauté on the Instant Pot, add the oil and heat for 1 or 2 minutes. Cook the chicken in batches, uncovered, until lightly browned, turning once, about 6 minutes per batch. Transfer the chicken to a plate.

3. To the pot, add the onion and bell pepper; cook for 1 minute, stirring the bottom of the pot to scrape up any browned bits. Stir in the rice, garlic, oregano, cayenne and ½ teaspoon salt and cook for 30 seconds, stirring. Stir in the broth.

4. Return the chicken to the pot, pushing it down into the rice mixture to submerge it. Cover and lock the lid. Cook on high pressure for 8 minutes. Use the quick release method.

5. Remove the lid and sprinkle the peas on top. Replace the lid, keeping it slightly ajar, and let everything stand 10 minutes. Remove the chicken and rice to a platter and sprinkle with olives and cilantro. Serve with lemon wedges.

PER SERVING *About 400 calories, 9 g fat (2 g saturated fat), 27 g protein, 876 mg sodium, 51 g carbohydrates, 3 g fiber*

2 tablespoons olive oil

2½ pounds lean beef stew meat, cut into 2-inch pieces

Kosher salt and pepper

2 tablespoons all-purpose flour

2 cups stout beer (such as Guinness Extra Stout)

1 6-ounce can tomato paste

3 medium onions, cut into 1-inch wedges

4 garlic cloves, smashed

8 thyme sprigs, tied together

1 small rutabaga (about 1 pound), cut into 1-inch pieces

4 medium carrots, cut into 2-inch pieces

2 medium parsnips, cut into 1-inch pieces

½ cup chopped fresh flat-leaf parsley

Mashed potatoes, for serving (optional)

Guinness Beef Stew

ACTIVE TIME 30 min. | **TOTAL TIME** 5 hr. 30 min. or 8 hr. 30 min. | **SERVES** 6

1. Press Sauté on the Instant Pot and heat 1 tablespoon oil. Season the beef with ½ teaspoon each salt and pepper. In batches, cook the beef, turning occasionally, until browned, 4 to 5 minutes; transfer to a plate and sprinkle with the flour.

2. To the Instant Pot add the beer, tomato paste and ¼ teaspoon each salt and pepper and whisk to combine. Add the onions, garlic, thyme, beef and any juices that have accumulated on the plate. Toss the ingredients together to combine.

3. Scatter the rutabaga, carrots and parsnips on top. Cover, lock the lid and cook on high pressure for 35 minutes. Let the pressure release naturally for 10 minutes, then release any remaining pressure.

4. Fold in the parsley and serve with mashed potatoes if desired.

PER SERVING *About 445 calories, 17 g fat (6 g saturated fat), 44 g protein, 460 mg sodium, 33 g carbohydrates, 7 g fiber*

Quick Mashed Potatoes

1. In the Instant Pot, combine 3 pounds potatoes and 1 cup water. Cover, lock the lid and cook on high pressure for 8 minutes. Use the quick release.

2. Drain the potatoes and return them to the pot. Add 4 tablespoons butter and 1½ teaspoons Kosher salt and mash the potatoes. Gradually add ¾ cup warm whole milk, continuing to mash the potatoes until smooth and fluffy.

3 tablespoons butter, softened, divided

2 stalks celery, finely chopped

1 large green bell pepper, finely chopped

1 medium onion, finely chopped

1½ teaspoons Creole seasoning

1 8-ounce bottle clam juice

2 medium tomatoes, coarsely chopped

2 tablespoons all-purpose flour

1½ pounds peeled, deveined large (25 to 30 count) shrimp

1 tablespoon Worcestershire sauce

1 tablespoon Louisiana-style hot sauce, or more to taste

¾ teaspoon kosher salt or more to taste

3 cups cooked white rice, for serving

Saucy Shrimp Creole

ACTIVE TIME 20 min. | **TOTAL TIME** 50 min. | **SERVES** 4

1. Press Sauté on the Instant Pot, add 1 tablespoon butter and heat until melted, 1 or 2 minutes. Add the celery, bell pepper and onion and cook until softened, stirring occasionally, 3 minutes. Stir in the Creole seasoning. Add the clam juice and top it all with the tomatoes; do not stir.

2. Cover and lock the lid. Cook on high pressure for 5 minutes. Meanwhile, mix the remaining 2 tablespoons butter and the flour on a plate using a fork to make a smooth paste.

3. Use the quick release method. Press Sauté and bring the vegetables to a simmer. Stir in the flour mixture; simmer the sauce, stirring, until thickened, about 1 minute.

4. Stir in the shrimp, Worcestershire sauce, hot sauce and salt. Replace the lid to slightly ajar and simmer until the shrimp are just opaque, stirring occasionally, about 3 minutes.

5. With potholders, remove the pot insert and stop cooking. Cover and let stand 1 minute. Taste and add additional hot sauce and/or salt if needed. Serve over rice.

PER SERVING *About 327 calories, 11 g fat (6 g saturated fat), 27 g protein, 1,911 mg sodium, 30 g carbohydrates, 3 g fiber*

1 tablespoon olive oil

8 ounces cremini mushrooms, sliced

1 medium onion, thinly sliced

3 garlic cloves, thinly sliced

2 tablespoons all-purpose flour

1 28-ounce can diced tomatoes

1¼ teaspoons dried oregano

¼ teaspoon salt

¼ teaspoon red pepper flakes

4 bone-in skinless chicken thighs
(about 8 ounces each)

1 medium red bell pepper, thinly sliced

3 tablespoons chopped rosemary

1 teaspoon balsamic vinegar

Grated Parmesan cheese, for topping

Prepared polenta, for serving

‹ Chicken Cacciatore

ACTIVE TIME 10 min. | **TOTAL TIME** 35 min. | **SERVES** 4

1. Press Sauté on the Instant Pot and adjust the heat to More. Add the oil and mushrooms and cook, uncovered, for 4 minutes. Stir in the onion and garlic and cook until the onions soften, about 4 minutes. Sprinkle in the flour and stir. Add the tomatoes, oregano, salt and red pepper flakes. Stir and scrape up any browned bits from the bottom of the pot.

2. Add the chicken thighs, pressing them into the sauce. Cover and lock the lid. Cook on high pressure for 9 minutes. Use the quick release method. Transfer the chicken to a plate. Stir and scrape any browned bits off the bottom of the pan.

3. Press Sauté and adjust the heat to More. Stir in the bell pepper and cook until just tender, about 4 minutes. Stir in the basil and vinegar. Serve with Parmesan.

PER SERVING *About 308 calories, 10 g fat (2 g saturated fat), 33 g protein, 573 mg sodium, 20 g carbohydrates, 3 g fiber*

---

1 large bunch fresh cilantro

1 tablespoon vegetable oil

3 pounds bone-in pork-shoulder
roast (Boston butt), well trimmed

1 16- to 18-ounce jar mild
salsa verde, divided

3 garlic cloves, halved lengthwise

2 pounds small red potatoes
(about 8), cut into quarters

Tomatillo Pork

ACTIVE TIME 10 min. | **TOTAL TIME** 1 hr. 20 min. | **SERVES** 4

1. From the cilantro, finely chop 1½ tablespoons of cilantro stems. Remove enough leaves from the remaining bunch to loosely pack ½ cup. Keep the leaves separate from the stems.

2. Press Sauté on the Instant Pot and adjust the heat to More. Heat the oil for 1 to 2 minutes. Add the pork and cook it, uncovered, until browned on all sides, 10 minutes. Add 1 cup of the salsa, the garlic and chopped cilantro to the pot.

3. Cover and lock the lid. Cook on high pressure for 45 minutes. Use the natural release method for 20 minutes and then release any remaining pressure.

4. Transfer the pork to a cutting board. Add the potatoes to the pot. Cover and lock the lid. Cook on high pressure for 5 minutes. Use the quick release method. Meanwhile, slice the pork against the grain and place it on a platter. Cover to keep warm. Using a slotted spoon, transfer the potatoes to the platter.

5. Skim off the fat from the broth in the pot and discard. Press Sauté and adjust the heat to More. Simmer for 10 minutes, or until the liquid is reduced by about one-third. Stir in the remaining salsa. Spoon the sauce over the pork and potatoes and scatter the cilantro leaves on top.

PER SERVING *About 355 calories, 16 g fat (5 g saturated fat), 28 g protein, 540 mg sodium, 22 g carbohydrates, 2 g fiber*

Cuban-Style Pulled Pork with Olives

1¼ cups low-sodium beef broth

2 green bell peppers, sliced

1 large onion, chopped

¼ cup tomato paste

3 garlic cloves, chopped

¾ teaspoon kosher salt

1 tablespoon ground cumin, divided

1 tablespoon dried oregano, divided

1 boneless pork shoulder (about 4 pounds), trimmed and cut into 3-inch pieces

1 cup pimiento-stuffed olives, sliced

1 tablespoon distilled white vinegar

Cilantro leaves, for topping

8 cups cooked yellow rice, for serving

ACTIVE TIME 15 min. | **TOTAL TIME** 2 hr. 20 min. | **SERVES** 6

1. Combine the broth and bell peppers in the Instant Pot. Cover and lock the lid. Cook on high pressure for 0 minutes. Use the quick release method. Using a slotted spoon, transfer the bell peppers to a bowl.

2. Add the onion, tomato paste, garlic, salt, 2½ teaspoons of the cumin and 2½ teaspoons of the oregano to the pot and stir to combine. Add the pork and press down to submerge in the liquid.

3. Cover and lock the lid. Cook on high pressure for 50 minutes. Use the natural release function for 15 minutes, then release any remaining pressure.

4. Transfer the pork to a cutting board. Skim off and discard any fat in the pot. Using two forks, break up the meat into pieces. Add the pork back to the pot along with the olives, vinegar, the remaining ½ teaspoon cumin and ½ teaspoon oregano and the cooked bell peppers. Cover and let stand 5 minutes or until heated through. Top with cilantro and serve with yellow rice.

PER SERVING *About 327 calories, 11 g fat (6 g saturated fat), 27 g protein, 1,911 mg sodium, 30 g carbohydrates, 3 g fiber*

Barbecue Ribs

2 tablespoons brown sugar

2 tablespoons paprika

½ teaspoon dried oregano

½ teaspoon cayenne

Kosher salt

1 2½- to 3½-pound rack St. Louis–style ribs, membrane removed

½ cup barbecue sauce, plus more for serving

ACTIVE TIME 20 min. | **TOTAL TIME** 1 hr. 10 min. | **SERVES** 4

1. In a medium bowl, combine the brown sugar, paprika, oregano, cayenne and ¾ teaspoon salt. Rub all over the ribs. Cut the rack into 4 pieces (about 5 ribs per piece).

2. Place the steamer rack or basket in the bottom of an Instant Pot and add ½ cup water. Place the ribs on top of the rack, lock the lid and cook on high pressure for 35 minutes. Use the quick release method to release the pressure, then open the lid.

3. Optional: Heat the grill to medium-high. Transfer the ribs to the grill, meaty side up, and brush with the sauce. Grill, covered, for 3 minutes. Turn and continue grilling, brushing with the sauce, and turning until the ribs are charred and glazed in some places, 3 to 5 minutes more.

PER SERVING *About 623 calories, 41 g fat (15 g saturated fat), 39 g protein, 837 mg sodium, 23 g carbohydrates, 2 g fiber*

Chapter 7

The Slow Cooker

The slow cooker is simply a classic. This trusty appliance has been making it easier to get dinner on the table with minimum fuss for decades. It has stood the test of time and definitely earned a spot in regular rotation. The slow cooker is a favorite because it cuts out any last-minute kitchen prep and allows you to skip right to the fun part: coming home to a house that smells amazing and a meal that's ready to eat.

What is a slow cooker?

Slow cookers are nifty appliances that cook hands-off, so you can whip up scrumptious meals without spending hours working in front of a stove. Once you've done your prep and put the ingredients into the cooker, it will cook the food at a steady and controlled temperature over a long period of time. There's no need to worry about this drying out your food, as the lid locks in moisture for soft and flavorful results.

They aren't just for stews and casseroles. In fact, they're real multitaskers, up to the task of cooking a cut of meat like a brisket or roast. Vegetarian family favorites like chili are also a go-to.

What are the benefits of slow cooking?

There are a number of benefits to using a slow cooker, but one of their main plus points is that they're highly convenient—you don't even need to check and stir your ingredients.

Cooking for a long time at a low temperature also helps tenderize meat and bring out its flavor, so you can get the best out of less-expensive cuts. You also preserve nutrients that are sometimes lost when cooking via other methods. Slow cookers use less electricity than an oven, too, and they won't heat up your kitchen.

How does a slow cooker work?

Traditional slow cookers have high and low settings. The high temperature usually cooks around 212°F, while the low hovers above 200°F. Some slow cookers also have a "keep warm" setting (165°F), which is above the food-safe temperature of 145°F but won't overcook the food. Newer models can brown and others have specific settings for rice and even sous vide. Not having to take out an extra pan to perform these tasks saves time and cleanup! The newest way to slow cook is in a multicooker that can also pressure cook (see Chapter 6).

Large cuts of meat, like pork shoulder for pulled pork, cook well in a slow cooker because the tough muscle fibers break down over time, allowing the meat to get nice and tender. Stews also work well because cheaper cuts of meat benefit from low and slow cooking, and you can control when you add the vegetables so they won't get overcooked.

How to Choose a Slow Cooker

:::::::::::::::::::::::::::

We've picked out the most important features to look out for when shopping for the best slow cooker for you.

What size do I need?
Slow cookers range in capacity, from a compact 1½ quarts up to 7 quarts. As a general guide, a 1½-quart to 2½-quart capacity is great for two people, a larger 4- to 4½-quart slow cooker will feed four and 5½ to 7 quarts is ideal for four to six people.

What features should I look for?
Slow cookers are available with all sorts of bells and whistles these days. Here are a few of the most popular features.

Timer This will come in handy if you're out for the day. Once the timer you set has been reached, the cooker will either switch off or automatically shift to the "keep warm" setting, depending on the model, so you come home to dinner that's ready to serve.

Keep warm This function can be found on the majority of slow cookers. It retains the temperature of your food without cooking it further. Some slow cookers will automatically shift to this mode after a program has ended, while others require switching manually.

Sous vide This feature mimics the increasingly popular way of cooking; sous vide is a French term that simply means "under vacuum." You place your food inside a sealed pouch and then pop it into a temperature-controlled water bath. The sealed pouch means the juices and subtle flavors that would otherwise be lost during conventional cooking are retained.

Transparent glass lid It's a good idea for your slow cooker to have a transparent glass lid, so you can keep a watchful eye on your food. The last thing you want is to be lifting the lid every now and then to check progress, as heat and steam will quickly escape, lengthening your cooking time.

Should I look for a model with a ceramic or metal insert?
Ceramic pots tend to be heavier than their stainless steel or aluminum counterparts, while the nonstick coating found on aluminum pots makes them easier to wash by hand. This needn't be a big concern as most of the pots we've tested are dishwasher-safe.

CIDER-BRAISED
POT ROAST
235

GH
KITCHEN
APPLIANCES
LAB

TOP-TESTED SLOW COOKERS

At the Good Housekeeping Institute, we test every slow cooker using both their high and low settings. We also measure the moisture lost when cooking to make sure meals don't end up tasting dry. We taste the end result of every dish to make sure food is perfectly cooked.

During our side-by-side analysis, our culinary experts tested slow cookers by making beef stew to chicken soup to roast beef. We made 72 servings of beef stew, cooked up 28 whole chickens, simmered 13 pounds of onions, 14 pounds of celery and 16 pounds of carrots all over the span of 432 hours. We checked for good temperature control (by measuring the temperature with a thermometer throughout the cook time) and consistency during cooking and evaluated each slow cooker's design, safety features and ease of use without the help of an instruction manual. We also assessed the "keep warm" function, meat tenderness and flavor development of dishes. What we found out impressed us: traditional slow cookers performed well and were consistent. Pressure cooker models that have slow cook features did well also, but with slightly lower results.

BEST OVERALL
All-Clad Deluxe Slow Cooker

All-Clad's top-of-the-line cooker features a nonstick cast-aluminum insert that you can use on the stovetop to brown ingredients before transferring it to the base for slow cooking.

Push-button controls and an easy-to-read digital display eliminate guesswork.

SCAN FOR
MORE INSTANT POT
LAB REVIEWS

SLOW COOKER SAFETY TIPS

Follow these simple safety tips and we have no doubt you'll be in good hands cooking "low and slow."

1. Inspect the cord every time you use your slow cooker.

2. Before you plug it in, take a minute to check both ends of the cord for any frayed or exposed wires. If you spot any, cut the cord and dispose of your appliance immediately—electrical tape is not a safe remedy.

3. Store and use your slow cooker on a flat, stable surface.

4. Make sure the exterior isn't close to any objects, especially flammable items like towels, curtains or cooking oil. There shouldn't be anything underneath it, and be sure it's nowhere near your sink or cooktop.

5. Unplug it when you're not using it, and make sure the cord is wrapped neatly and not folded up in a way that will expose wires.

6. Maintain extreme caution when accepting hand-me-down appliances. Though slow cookers have been around for a long time, technology has improved a lot in recent years. Older models don't offer modern safety features like auto shutoff. If you notice any off odors or see that the exterior of your slow cooker feels hotter than it should when in use, unplug it right away and toss it. If there's a chance your slow cooker has spent time in someone's garage, you should probably consider upgrading.

Cooking Tips for Best Results

1. **Add some color.** If you have time, browning your meat and vegetables in the cooking pot (if your slow cooker has a brown or sear setting) or a skillet beforehand will elevate your stew from okay to awesome.

2. **Take stock of your stock.** Because lids of slow cookers are more efficient than conventional casserole dishes at trapping steam in, liquid doesn't reduce naturally. Making sure not to add too much liquid at the beginning will help to concentrate the flavors.

3. **Feel the strain.** If you do find yourself with too much cooking liquid at the end, pour the stew through a colander into a wide pan (reserving all the meat and vegetables) and boil the juices over a high heat, sampling every so often until the taste is the intensity you desire.

4. **Reduce your booze.** Only add wine in the initial stages when you're browning the meat and vegetables; otherwise, it will burn off in the course of the cooking time.

5. **Add herbs for flavor.** For maximum flavor, add dried or woody herbs (like rosemary and thyme) at the beginning so that they can soften and release their fragrance and oils. Add tender fresh herbs like basil and cilantro—whose delicate aromas would be destroyed after hours of cooking—right before serving.

6. **Remember the fifth element.** Umami-packed condiments are the slow cooker's best friend. Worcestershire sauce adds lift to a dish that has been simmering for hours while soy sauce intensifies tomato dishes.

7. **Be sweet.** Sugar enhances savory foods and adds the final dimension that is often missing. A small amount of brown sugar, honey, or fruit preserves balances out the flavors and complements both meat and vegetable recipes.

8. **Meat first.** Add browned meat and large chunks of root vegetables first, softer vegetables and carbs in last (or on the side). That way everything softens perfectly without overcooking.

9. **Get thrifty.** Cheaper cuts of meat are transformed when slow cooked, especially if you've taken the time to brown the roast beforehand. The gelatin released as the sinew breaks down during the long cooking time enriches and thickens the cooking liquid too.

10. **Keep a lid on it.** Don't be tempted to lift the lid every half hour. Each time you do, the temperature of the mixture drops significantly and the slow cooker takes ages to heat back up, adding extra cooking time.

½ cup dry red wine

2 tablespoons all-purpose flour

2 tablespoons tomato paste

2 teaspoons low-sodium beef bouillon base (we used Better Than Bouillon)

12 ounces small yellow potatoes (about 10), halved

1 14-ounce package frozen pearl onions

4 large carrots, cut into 2-inch pieces

4 garlic cloves, smashed

8 thyme sprigs

2 bay leaves (optional)

1½ pounds lean beef brisket

Kosher salt and pepper

Chopped fresh flat-leaf parsley, for topping (optional)

◂ Beef Bourguignon Brisket

ACTIVE TIME 15 min. | **TOTAL TIME** 5 hr. 15 min. or 8 hr. 15 min. | **SERVES** 4

1. In a 5- to 6-quart slow cooker, whisk together the wine, flour, tomato paste and bouillon base. Add the potatoes, onions, carrots, garlic, thyme and bay leaves, if using.

2. Season the beef with ½ teaspoon each salt and pepper and nestle among the vegetables. Cook, covered, until the beef is tender, 7 to 8 hours on low or 4 to 5 hours on high.

3. Discard the thyme and bay leaves and transfer the brisket to a cutting board. Slice the brisket and serve with the vegetables and any juices. Sprinkle with parsley if desired.

PER SERVING About 452 calories, 16.5 g fat (6.5 g saturated fat), 39 g protein, 565 mg sodium, 38 g carbohydrates, 5 g fiber

1 bone-in chicken breast (1½ pounds), split, skin removed

4 carrots, halved crosswise

1 medium onion, quartered

1 lemon, halved

4 dill sprigs, plus more for topping

4 flat-leaf parsley sprigs

4 cups low-sodium chicken broth

2 stalks celery

¾ cup orzo

8 ounces snap peas, thinly sliced crosswise

Lemony Chicken & Orzo Soup

ACTIVE TIME 20 min. | **TOTAL TIME** 5 hr. 40 min. or 8 hr. 40 min. | **SERVES** 4

1. Place the chicken, carrots, onion and lemon in a 5- to 6-quart slow cooker. Using kitchen string, tie the dill and parsley together and nestle it among the chicken and vegetables. Add the broth and 2 cups water, cover, and cook until the chicken is cooked through and easily shreds, 7 to 8 hours on low or 4 to 5 hours on high.

2. Thirty minutes before serving, transfer the chicken to a bowl and the carrots and onion to a cutting board. Discard the lemon and herbs. Strain the liquid if desired and return it to the slow cooker.

3. Cut the celery into ¼-inch pieces and add it to the slow cooker along with the orzo. Cover and cook on high until the orzo is tender, 20 to 25 minutes.

4. Meanwhile, cut the carrots into rounds and cut the onion into ¼-inch pieces. Shred the chicken into large pieces, discarding the bones.

5. Just before serving, return the chicken, carrots and onion to the slow cooker along with the snap peas and cook for 3 minutes. Serve with extra dill if desired.

PER SERVING About 316 calories, 4 g fat (1 g saturated fat), 31 g protein, 268 mg sodium, 39 g carbohydrates, 5 g fiber

1 28-ounce can fire-roasted crushed tomatoes

1 14½-ounce can no-salt-added petite diced tomatoes

1 tablespoon chili powder

2 teaspoons ground cumin

2 large carrots, cut into ¼-inch pieces

1 onion, chopped

1 poblano pepper, cut into ¼-inch pieces

¾ cup wheat berries

2 garlic cloves, finely chopped

Kosher salt and pepper

2 15½-ounce cans low-sodium kidney, pinto, or black beans, rinsed

1 cup frozen corn, thawed

Shredded Cheddar cheese, sour cream and scallions, for topping (optional)

‹ Chili with Wheat Berries, Beans & Corn

ACTIVE TIME 20 min. | **TOTAL TIME** 6 hr. 20 min. or 8 hr. 20 min. | **SERVES** 4

1. In a 5- to 6-quart slow cooker, stir together the tomatoes (and their juice), chili powder and cumin. Add the carrots, onion, poblano pepper, wheat berries, garlic and ½ teaspoon each salt and pepper. Cook, covered, until the wheat berries are cooked but still chewy, 7 to 8 hours on low or 5 to 6 hours on high.

2. Ten minutes before serving, gently stir in the beans and corn and cook until heated through.

3. Ladle the chili into bowls and top with the Cheddar, sour cream and scallions if desired.

PER SERVING *About 483 calories, 2 g fat (.5 g saturated fat), 24 g protein, 860 mg sodium, 94 g carbohydrates, 26 g fiber*

MAKE IT VEGAN Omit Cheddar and sour cream or use a dairy-free alternative.

2 pounds boneless beef chuck, trimmed of excess fat and cut into 1½-inch pieces

1 large onion, chopped

1 to 2 jalapeños, seeded, if desired, and sliced

6 garlic cloves, finely chopped

2 tablespoons lime juice, plus lime wedges for serving

1 tablespoon chili powder

Kosher salt

¼ pound green beans, thinly sliced crosswise

1 10-ounce box couscous

½ cup sliced fresh basil

Chili-Spiced Braised Beef with Green Beans

ACTIVE TIME 10 min. | **TOTAL TIME** 5 hr. 10 min. or 8 hr. 10 min. | **SERVES** 4

1. In a 5- to 6-quart slow cooker, add the beef, onion, jalapeños, garlic, lime juice, chili powder and ½ teaspoon salt. Cook, covered, until the beef is very tender, 7 to 8 hours on low or 4 to 5 hours on high.

2. Stir in the green beans, cover, and cook for 3 minutes. Cook the couscous according to the package directions. Spoon the vegetables, beef and sauce over the couscous and sprinkle with the basil; serve with the lime wedges if desired.

PER SERVING *About 608 calories, 10 g fat (4 g saturated fat), 53 g protein, 452 mg sodium, 61 g carbohydrates, 6 g fiber*

1 8-ounce can tomato sauce

3 tablespoons cider vinegar, divided

2 tablespoons packed dark brown sugar

1 tablespoon Dijon mustard

2 teaspoons chili powder

1 teaspoon Worcestershire sauce

1 onion, sliced

4 garlic cloves, chopped

2 pounds lean beef brisket, trimmed of excess fat

Kosher salt and pepper

¼ cup low-fat sour cream

½ small head cabbage (green, red or a combination; about 1 pound)

4 buns, split

Sliced pickles and potato chips, for serving (optional)

‹ Barbecue Brisket Sandwiches with Quick Coleslaw

ACTIVE TIME 25 min. | **TOTAL TIME** 6 hr. 25 min. or 8 hr. 25 min. | **SERVES** 4

1. In a 5- to 6-quart slow cooker, whisk together the tomato sauce, 2 tablespoons of the vinegar, the brown sugar, mustard, chili powder and Worcestershire sauce. Add the onion and garlic and toss to combine.

2. Season the brisket with ½ teaspoon pepper, then cut crosswise into 2½-inch pieces. Add the meat to the slow cooker and turn to coat. Cook, covered, until the meat is tender and easily pulls apart, 7 to 8 hours on low or 5 to 6 hours on high.

3. Thirty minutes before the beef is done, in a large bowl, whisk together the sour cream, remaining tablespoon vinegar and ¼ teaspoon salt. Cut the cabbage in half, core and thinly slice. Add the cabbage to the bowl and toss to coat.

4. Using two forks, shred the beef, then stir it into the cooking liquid. Serve the beef and onions on the buns, topped with coleslaw, pickles and chips if desired.

PER SERVING *About 526 calories, 13.5 g fat (5 g saturated fat), 58 g protein, 886 mg sodium, 43 g carbohydrates, 5 g fiber*

1 8-ounce can tomato sauce

1 tablespoon chopped chipotle in adobo, plus 1 tablespoon adobo sauce

2 teaspoons ground cumin

Kosher salt

1 pound flank steak, cut crosswise into 2-inch-wide pieces

1 red onion, thinly sliced

4 garlic cloves, pressed

Corn tortillas, sour cream and pico de gallo, for serving

≡ FAMILY FRIENDLY ≡

Smoky Beef Tacos

ACTIVE TIME 15 min. | **TOTAL TIME** 5 hr. 15 min. or 8 hr. 15 min. | **SERVES** 8

1. Combine the tomato sauce, chipotle, adobo sauce, cumin and ½ tsp salt in a 5- to 6-quart slow cooker. Stir in the steak, onion and garlic. Cover and cook until the meat is very tender, 4 to 5 hours on high or 7 to 8 hours on low. Shred the beef with two forks.

2. Serve with tortillas, sour cream, and pico de gallo.

PER SERVING *About 175 calories, 7.5 g fat (3 g saturated fat), 22 g protein, 340 mg sodium, 4 g carbohydrates, 1 g fiber*

TIP To easily warm corn tortillas, wrap up to six in a damp towel and microwave on high until soft and pliable, about 20 seconds.

1 15-ounce can crushed tomatoes

3 large garlic cloves, finely chopped

1 tablespoon tomato paste

1 teaspoon dried oregano

1 tablespoon sugar

1 bunch scallions, thinly sliced, divided

Kosher salt and pepper

4 large bell peppers (red, orange,
   yellow or a mix)

¾ pound lean ground beef
   (at least 90 percent)

¾ cup uncooked instant brown rice

2 tablespoons raisins,
   roughly chopped

2 tablespoons crumbled
   feta cheese

Beef & Rice Stuffed Peppers

ACTIVE TIME 15 min. | **TOTAL TIME** 4 hr. 15 min. or 5 hr. 15 min. | **SERVES** 4

1. In a bowl, stir together the tomatoes, garlic, tomato paste, oregano, sugar, all but ¼ cup of the scallions and ½ teaspoon pepper. Transfer half of the mixture (about 1 cup) to a 5- to 6-quart slow cooker.

2. Slice the tops off the peppers just below the stems. Roughly chop the tops and add to the bowl with the remaining sauce, along with the beef, rice, raisins and ½ teaspoon salt; mix to combine.

3. Remove the ribs and seeds from the peppers. Slice a very thin piece from the base of each pepper so they sit upright and flat, but do not cut through. Season the inside of the peppers with ¼ teaspoon each salt and pepper, then stuff with the beef mixture (about 1 cup per pepper).

4. Transfer the peppers to the slow cooker, cover and cook until the peppers are tender and the rice is cooked through, 3 to 4 hours on high or 5 hours on low.

5. Transfer the peppers to plates. Stir the sauce to incorporate any excess liquid. Spoon the sauce over the peppers and sprinkle with the feta and remaining scallions.

PER SERVING *About 358 calories, 10 g fat (4 g saturated fat), 23 g protein, 500 mg sodium, 44 g carbohydrates, 5 g fiber*

TIP Try another topping: Toss ¼ cup sliced almonds with 1 teaspoon olive oil and ¼ teaspoon ground cumin and bake at 400°F until golden brown, 5 to 6 minutes, then sprinkle over the peppers.

¼ cup low-sodium soy sauce

¼ cup honey

6 garlic cloves, finely chopped

1 tablespoon grated peeled
   fresh ginger

1 to 2 teaspoons chili garlic sauce

¼ teaspoon ground cinnamon

1½ pounds flank steak, cut crosswise
   into 2½-inch-thick strips

4 scallions

½ small head iceberg lettuce, thinly
   sliced (about 4 cups)

½ cup cilantro leaves

1 tablespoon rice vinegar

8 small flour tortillas

Toasted sesame seeds (optional)

‹ Honey-Soy Steak Tacos

ACTIVE TIME 20 min. | **TOTAL TIME** 5 hr. 20 min. or 7 hr. 20 min. | **SERVES** 4

1. In a 5- to 6-quart slow cooker, combine the soy sauce, honey, garlic, ginger, chili garlic sauce and cinnamon. Add the steak and turn to coat. Cover and cook until the meat shreds easily, 7 to 8 hours on low or 5 to 6 hours on high.

2. Fifteen minutes before serving, thinly slice scallions lengthwise and cut into 2½-inch pieces. In a large bowl, toss the scallions with the lettuce, cilantro and vinegar.

3. Remove the beef from the slow cooker and serve it in tortillas, topped with the lettuce mixture. Sprinkle with the sesame seeds, if using.

PER SERVING *About 542 calories, 17 g fat (10 g saturated fat), 42 g protein, 1,081 mg sodium, 51 g carbohydrates, 4 g fiber*

TIP To toast sesame seeds, heat a skillet on medium; add the seeds and cook, stirring constantly, until golden brown. Transfer immediately to a plate (they will continue to cook).

¾ cup light coconut milk

1 to 2 tablespoons red curry paste

2 garlic cloves, finely chopped

2 teaspoons grated peeled
   fresh ginger

Kosher salt

1 pound lean beef stew meat, trimmed
   and cut into 1-inch pieces

8 ounces rice noodles

3 ounces snap peas, sliced crosswise

½ red onion, thinly sliced

2 tablespoons lime juice, plus lime
   wedges for serving

½ cup cilantro or basil leaves

Chopped peanuts, for
   topping (optional)

Coconut Beef with Rice Noodles

ACTIVE TIME 15 min. | **TOTAL TIME** 5 hr. 15 min. or 7 hr. 15 min. | **SERVES** 4

1. In a 5- to 6-quart slow cooker, whisk together the coconut milk, curry paste, garlic, ginger and ¼ teaspoon salt. Add the beef and toss to coat. Cook, covered, until the meat easily pulls apart, 6 to 7 hours on low or 4 to 5 hours on high.

2. Before serving, place rice noodles in a bowl and cover with bowling water. Let sit until soft and pliable, 8 to 15 minutes (times will differ depending on noodle type and thickness). Gently fold the peas, onion and lime juice into the beef mixture and cook for 3 minutes. Fold in the cilantro. Serve the beef mixture over the noodles. Sprinkle with chopped peanuts (if using) and serve with lime wedges if desired.

PER SERVING *About 491 calories, 11 g fat (5 g saturated fat), 39 g protein, 242 mg sodium, 55 g carbohydrates, 1 g fiber*

½ cup apricot jam

¼ cup ketchup

2 tablespoons reduced-sodium
  soy sauce

1 tablespoon grated peeled
  fresh ginger

¼ teaspoon red pepper flakes

2 pounds boneless, skinless chicken
  thighs, trimmed

1 medium onion, chopped

2 garlic cloves, finely chopped

1 red bell pepper, sliced into
  ¼-inch pieces

Cooked long-grain white rice,
  for serving

Scallions and sesame seeds,
  for topping (optional)

◄ Sesame Chicken

ACTIVE TIME 20 min. | **TOTAL TIME** 4 hr. 50 min. or 6 hr. 50 min. | **SERVES** 4

1. In a 5- to 6-quart slow cooker, combine the apricot jam, ketchup, soy sauce, ginger and red pepper flakes. Add the chicken, onion and garlic and toss to coat.

2. Scatter the bell pepper over the top and cook, covered, until the chicken is cooked through, 5 to 6 hours on low or 3 to 4 hours on high.

3. Serve the chicken and sauce on top of the rice and sprinkle with scallions and sesame seeds if desired.

PER SERVING *About 588 calories, 10 g fat (2 g saturated fat), 50 g protein, 814 mg sodium, 76 g carbohydrates, 1 g fiber*

TIP Some jams and soy sauces can contain gluten. To ensure a gluten-free dinner, purchase varieties that don't contain wheat or wheat-derived glucose syrup, or ones that aren't processed on machinery alongside wheat, barley, rye, triticale or malt.

1 15-ounce container part-skim
  ricotta cheese

8 ounces part-skim mozzarella cheese,
  shredded (2 cups), divided

¼ cup grated Parmesan cheese
  (about 1 ounce)

Kosher salt and pepper

2 cups baby spinach, roughly chopped

¾ pound lean ground beef (at least
  90 percent lean)

2 garlic cloves, finely chopped

½ teaspoon dried oregano

1 26-ounce jar marinara sauce, divided

12 dry lasagna noodles (from a
  1-pound box)

≡ FAMILY FRIENDLY ≡

Beef & Spinach Lasagna

ACTIVE TIME 20 min. | **TOTAL TIME** 2 hr. 20 min. or 4 hr. 20 min. | **SERVES** 6

1. In a medium bowl, combine the ricotta, 1 cup of the mozzarella, the Parmesan and ¼ teaspoon each salt and pepper; fold in the spinach.

2. In a 5- to 6-quart slow cooker, combine the beef, garlic, oregano, ½ teaspoon salt and ¼ teaspoon pepper. Transfer half of the meat mixture to a small bowl. Add ½ cup of the marinara sauce to the slow cooker and mix into the meat; spread the meat evenly on the bottom of the slow cooker.

3. Top with a layer of the noodles, breaking them to fit as necessary. Spread one-third of the remaining sauce (¾ cup) over the noodles and dollop with one-third of the ricotta mixture (1 cup) and half the remaining meat; repeat.

4. Top with a layer of noodles, the remaining sauce and the remaining ricotta mixture. Sprinkle with the remaining mozzarella and cook, covered, on low for 4 hours or on high for 2 hours.

PER SERVING *About 613 calories, 24 g fat (12 g saturated fat), 40 g protein, 1,172 mg sodium, 57 g carbohydrates, 5 g fiber*

- 1 28-ounce can diced tomatoes, drained
- 2 tablespoons tomato paste
- 2 tablespoons grated peeled fresh ginger
- 1 tablespoon curry powder
- Kosher salt and pepper
- 1½ pounds boneless, skinless chicken thighs, trimmed and halved lengthwise
- 1 small head cauliflower (about 1¾ pounds), cored and cut into small florets
- 1 medium onion, finely chopped
- ¼ cup golden raisins
- Cooked long-grain white rice, for serving
- ½ cup roughly chopped fresh cilantro
- Greek yogurt and lemon wedges, for serving (optional)

‹ Indian Spiced Chicken & Cauliflower

ACTIVE TIME 20 min. | **TOTAL TIME** 5 hr. 20 min. or 7 hr. 20 min. | **SERVES** 4

1. In a 5- to 6-quart slow cooker, whisk together the tomatoes, tomato paste, ginger, curry powder, ½ teaspoon salt and ¼ teaspoon pepper.

2. Add the chicken, cauliflower, onion and raisins to the slow cooker and stir to combine. Cook, covered, until the chicken is cooked through, 4 to 5 hours on high or 6 to 7 hours on low.

3. Spoon the chicken mixture over the rice and top with the cilantro. Serve with yogurt and lemon wedges if desired.

PER SERVING *About 495 calories, 8 g fat (2 g saturated fat), 40 g protein, 726 mg sodium, 64 g carbohydrates, 5 g fiber*

TIP Keep this recipe quick and easy by using precooked rice.

- 1 large orange
- ¼ cup packed dark brown sugar
- ¼ cup red wine vinegar
- Kosher salt and pepper
- 8 pieces bone-in, dark meat chicken (thighs and drumsticks, about 2½ pounds total), skin removed
- 2 tablespoons all-purpose flour
- 6 garlic cloves, smashed
- 1 large red onion, cut into ½-inch-thick wedges
- 1 15¼-ounce can peach halves, drained and cut into 1-inch pieces
- ½ cup roughly chopped fresh flat-leaf parsley
- Cooked long-grain white rice, for serving

Sweet & Sour Chicken

ACTIVE TIME 15 min. | **TOTAL TIME** 6 hr. 15 min. or 8 hr. 15 min. | **SERVES** 4

1. Using a vegetable peeler, remove 2 strips of zest from the orange. Thinly slice the zest and set aside. Juice the orange into a 5- to 6-quart slow cooker (you should have about ½ cup). Whisk in the brown sugar, vinegar, ¾ teaspoon salt and ¼ teaspoon pepper.

2. Toss the chicken with the flour; add it to the slow cooker with the garlic and orange zest. Scatter the onion over the top. Cook, covered, until the chicken is cooked through and the sauce has slightly thickened, 7 to 8 hours on low or 5 to 6 hours on high.

3. Transfer chicken to a platter. Add the peaches to the slow cooker and cook, covered, until heated through, about 3 minutes; fold in the parsley. Spoon the peach and onion mix over the chicken and serve with rice.

PER SERVING *About 549 calories, 7 g fat (2 g saturated fat), 38 g protein, 520 mg sodium, 81 g carbohydrates, 2 g fiber*

1/3 cup white wine

3 tablespoons red wine vinegar, divided

2 tablespoons brown sugar

1 teaspoon dried oregano

Kosher salt and pepper

1/2 cup prunes

1/3 cup pitted green olives

6 garlic cloves, smashed

1 tablespoon capers, drained

8 pieces bone-in dark meat chicken (thighs and drumsticks, about 2 1/2 pounds total), skin removed

1/4 cup chopped fresh flat-leaf parsley

Cooked long-grain white rice, for serving

◄ Chicken Marbella

ACTIVE TIME 15 min. | **TOTAL TIME** 4 hr. 15 min. or 6 hr. 15 min. | **SERVES** 4

1. In a 5- to 6-quart slow cooker, whisk together the wine, 2 tablespoons of the vinegar, brown sugar, oregano and 1/4 teaspoon each salt and pepper. Add the prunes, olives, garlic and capers and mix to combine.

2. Add the chicken, nestling it among the olives and prunes. Cover and cook until the meat is tender and cooked through, on low for 5 to 6 hours or on high for 3 to 4 hours.

3. Gently stir in the remaining tablespoon vinegar and the parsley. Serve the chicken, prunes, olives and cooking liquid over the rice.

PER SERVING *About 302 calories, 8 g fat (2 g saturated fat), 34 g protein, 487 mg sodium, 24 g carbohydrates, 2 g fiber*

TIP **Keep this recipe quick and easy by using precooked rice.**

3/4 cup light coconut milk

2 tablespoons creamy peanut butter

1 tablespoon red curry paste

1 teaspoon grated peeled fresh ginger

1 1/2 pounds boneless, skinless chicken thighs, cut into 1 1/2-inch pieces

2 red bell peppers, sliced 3/4 inch thick

1 large onion, sliced

1 pound rice noodles

1 cup frozen peas

1/4 cup cilantro leaves

Lime wedges, for serving (optional)

Coconut-Curry Chicken

ACTIVE TIME 15 min. | **TOTAL TIME** 4 hr. 15 min. or 6 hr. 15 min. | **SERVES** 6

1. In a 5- to 6-quart slow cooker, combine the coconut milk, peanut butter, curry paste and ginger; mix in the chicken, peppers and onion.

2. Cook, covered, until chicken is cooked through, 5 to 6 hours on low or 3 to 4 hours on high.

3. Before serving, place rice noodles in a bowl and cover with bowling water. Let sit until soft and pliable, 8 to 15 minutes (times will differ depending on noodle type and thickness). Stir the peas into the chicken mixture, and cook, covered, until heated through, about 3 minutes. Spoon the chicken, vegetables and sauce over the noodles and sprinkle with the cilantro; serve with the lime wedges if desired.

PER SERVING *About 506 calories, 9 g fat (3 g saturated fat), 26 g protein, 175 mg sodium, 78 g carbohydrates, 3 g fiber*

2 tablespoons tomato paste

2 teaspoons caraway seeds

2 teaspoons smoked paprika

3 cups beef broth (made with
1½ teaspoons low-sodium beef
bouillon; we used Better
Than Bouillon)

1 pound beef chuck, trimmed and cut
into ¾-inch pieces

2 tablespoons all-purpose flour

2 medium carrots, cut on a diagonal
into ½-inch-thick pieces

1 onion, finely chopped

2 garlic cloves, finely chopped

¼ small bunch flat-leaf parsley,
leaves and stems separated

½ cup couscous

Kosher salt and pepper

◂ Hearty Beef Soup

ACTIVE TIME 20 min. | **TOTAL TIME** 4 hr. or 7 hr. 30 min. | **SERVES** 4

1. In a 5- to 6-quart slow cooker, whisk together the tomato paste, caraway seeds and paprika. Gradually whisk in the broth.

2. Toss the beef with the flour and ½ teaspoon each salt and pepper. Add the beef to the pot along with the carrots, onion and garlic; toss to coat. Tie the parsley stems together with kitchen string and add to the pot. Cook, covered, until the meat is tender, 7 to 8 hours on low or 3½ to 4½ hours on high.

3. Fifteen minutes before serving, place couscous and ¼ teaspoon salt in a medium bowl and pour ⅔ cup just-boiled water on top. Cover and let sit until liquid has been absorbed and the couscous is tender, about 10 minutes, then fluff with a fork. Finely chop the parsley leaves and fold into the couscous.

4. Discard the parsley stems from the soup and ladle into bowls. Spoon couscous over the top.

PER SERVING *About 394 calories, 19 g fat (8 g saturated fat), 27 g protein, 661 mg sodium, 29 g carbohydrates, 4 g fiber*

1 28-ounce can no-salt-added
fire-roasted crushed tomatoes

1 14½-ounce can no-salt-added
petite diced tomatoes

1 tablespoon chili powder

2 teaspoons dried oregano

2 teaspoons ground cumin

Kosher salt and pepper

¾ cup wheat berries

1 large onion, chopped

1 poblano pepper, cut into
¼-inch pieces

2 large garlic cloves, pressed

2 15-ounce cans low-sodium beans
(such as kidney or pinto), rinsed

2 cups shredded cooked
white-meat chicken

1 cup frozen corn, thawed

Cilantro leaves, crumbled cotija
cheese and lime wedges, for
serving (optional)

≡ FAMILY FRIENDLY ≡

Tex-Mex Chicken Chili

ACTIVE TIME 20 min. | **TOTAL TIME** 4 hr. 40 min. or 7 hr. 40 min. | **SERVES** 4

1. In a 5- to 6-quart slow cooker, stir together the tomatoes (and their juice), chili powder, oregano, cumin, 1 cup water and ¼ teaspoon each salt and pepper.

2. Stir in the wheat berries, onion, poblano pepper and garlic. Cook, covered, until the wheat berries are tender but still a bit chewy, 7 to 8 hours on low or 4 to 5 hours on high.

3. Ten minutes before serving, gently stir in the beans, chicken and corn and cook until heated through. Serve topped with cilantro, cotija and lime wedges if desired.

PER SERVING *About 490 calories, 2.5 g fat (1 g saturated fat), 41 g protein, 460 mg sodium, 79 g carbohydrates, 19 g fiber*

2 tablespoons cowboy rub (like McCormick Grill Mates)

1 tablespoon dark brown sugar

2 teaspoons smoked paprika

1 teaspoon ground cumin

Kosher salt

1 6-pound flat-cut beef brisket

1 tablespoon olive oil

1 large sweet onion, sliced

3 garlic cloves, minced

1 cup chopped fresh cilantro

Tortillas, pico de gallo, crumbled queso fresco and lime wedges, for serving

◄ Cowboy Brisket Tacos

ACTIVE TIME 25 min. | **TOTAL TIME** 8 hr. 25 min. | **SERVES** 14

1. Stir together the cowboy rub, brown sugar, paprika, cumin and 1½ teaspoons salt. Trim the fat from the brisket, leaving a thin layer; cut into 3-inch chunks. Rub the brisket pieces evenly with the spice mixture. Lightly grease a 5- to 6-quart slow cooker with olive oil and add the onion and garlic. Arrange the meat on top and sprinkle with the cilantro.

2. Cover and cook on low 8 to 9 hours or until the brisket shreds easily with a fork. Remove the meat from the pot and drizzle with a small amount of the cooking liquid.

3. Serve the brisket on warm tortillas with your favorite toppings, such as pico de gallo, queso fresco and lime wedges.

PER SERVING *About 239 calories, 8 g fat (3 g saturated fat), 38 g protein, 174 mg sodium, 2 g carbohydrates, 0 g fiber*

---

1 cup apple cider

3 tablespoons tomato paste

2 tablespoons all-purpose flour

2 tablespoons Worcestershire sauce

Kosher salt and pepper

3 medium parsnips, quartered lengthwise and cut into 2-inch pieces

2 medium sweet potatoes (about 1 pound), cut into ½-inch-thick wedges

1 medium onion, cut into ½-inch-thick wedges

4 large garlic cloves, thinly sliced

2 rosemary sprigs

1 3-pound beef bottom round roast or chuck roast, trimmed of excess fat

Cider-Braised Pot Roast

ACTIVE TIME 15 min. | **TOTAL TIME** 7 hr. 15 min. or 9 hr. 15 min. | **SERVES** 6

1. In a 5- to 6-quart slow cooker, whisk together the cider, tomato paste, flour, Worcestershire sauce and ¼ teaspoon each salt and pepper. Add the parsnips, sweet potatoes, onion, garlic and rosemary and toss to combine.

2. Season the roast with 1 teaspoon each salt and pepper and nestle among the vegetables. Cook, covered, until the meat is tender, 6 to 7 hours on high or 8 to 9 hours on low.

3. Transfer the roast to a cutting board and slice. Serve with the vegetables and cooking juices.

PER SERVING *About 424 calories, 10 g fat (3 g saturated fat), 53 g protein, 620 mg sodium, 31 g carbohydrates, 5 g fiber*

1 large red onion

3 pounds boneless lamb shoulder, trimmed and cut into 2-inch pieces

1 tablespoon paprika

2 teaspoons ground cumin

1 teaspoon dried oregano

Kosher salt and pepper

4 garlic cloves, smashed

1/2 seedless cucumber

2 tablespoons lemon juice, plus lemon wedges for serving

1 tablespoon olive oil

8 ounces frozen French fries (optional)

4 pieces flatbread

Greek yogurt and chopped fresh mint, for serving (optional)

Lamb Souvlaki

ACTIVE TIME 20 min. | **TOTAL TIME** 5 hr. 20 min. or 7 hr. 20 min. | **SERVES** 4

1. Cut three-quarters of the onion into 1/2-inch-thick rings. Wrap and refrigerate the remaining onion until ready to serve.

2. In a 5- to 6-quart slow cooker, toss the lamb with the paprika, cumin, oregano and 1/2 teaspoon each salt and pepper. Toss with the garlic and 1/4 cup water. Place the sliced onion on top and cook, covered, until the lamb is tender and easily pulls apart, 6 to 7 hours on low or 4 to 5 hours on high.

3. Thirty minutes before serving, thinly slice the cucumber into half-moons and finely chop the reserved onion. In a bowl, toss together the cucumber, onion, lemon juice, oil and 1/4 teaspoon each salt and pepper. Cook fries according to package directions, if desired.

4. Transfer the onions from the slow cooker to a plate. Skim off and discard any fat that has risen to the top of the cooking liquid. Using a fork, break the lamb into pieces and toss with the cooking liquid to coat. Divide the lamb and onions among the flatbreads and top with the fries and cucumber mixture. Serve with the yogurt, mint and lemon wedges if desired.

PER SERVING *About 605 calories, 25 g fat (7 g saturated fat), 45 g protein, 728 mg sodium, 48 g carbohydrates, 4 g fiber*

TIP **You can substitute beef chuck or pork shoulder for the lamb.**

¼ cup reduced-sodium soy sauce

¼ cup plus 1 tablespoon
   honey, divided

3 tablespoons lime juice, divided

1 tablespoon Worcestershire sauce

1 large garlic clove, finely chopped

1½ pounds boneless pork butt or
   shoulder, trimmed and cut into
   1½-inch pieces

Kosher salt and pepper

3 tablespoons plain yogurt

1 tablespoon cider vinegar

¼ small head cabbage, shredded
   (about 3 cups)

¼ pineapple, cored and cut into
   ½-inch pieces

2 scallions, finely chopped

¼ cup chopped fresh cilantro

Cooked white rice, for serving

‹ Honey-Lime Pork with Pineapple Slaw

ACTIVE TIME 30 min. | **TOTAL TIME** 4 hr. 30 min. or 6 hr. 30 min. | **SERVES** 4

1. In a 5- to 6-quart slow cooker, whisk together the soy sauce, ¼ cup of the honey, 1 tablespoon of the lime juice and the Worcestershire sauce; stir in the garlic. Season the pork with ¼ teaspoon salt and ½ teaspoon pepper. Add the pork to the slow cooker and toss to coat. Cover and cook until the pork is tender and easily pulled apart with a fork, 4 to 5 hours on high or 6 to 7 hours on low.

2. Fifteen minutes before serving, in a large bowl, whisk together the yogurt, vinegar, remaining 2 tablespoons lime juice and tablespoon honey and a pinch each of salt and pepper. Add the cabbage, pineapple and scallions, and toss. Fold in the cilantro just before serving.

3. Transfer the pork to a bowl and, using two forks, break into smaller pieces. Serve over rice with the pineapple slaw.

PER SERVING *About 375 calories, 10.5 g fat (3.5 g saturated fat), 35 g protein, 895 mg sodium, 36 g carbohydrates, 2 g fiber*

TIP **Keep this recipe quick and easy by using precooked rice.**

---

4 ounces thick-cut bacon

2 cups low-sodium chicken broth

½ cup dry white wine

3 tablespoons tomato paste

1 14½-ounce can petite diced
   tomatoes, drained

1 medium onion, chopped

8 garlic cloves, smashed

2 pounds well-trimmed pork butt,
   trimmed and cut into 2-inch pieces
   (about 1¼ pounds total)

4 thyme sprigs

½ cup brown lentils, rinsed and
   picked over

1 15-ounce can small white
   beans, rinsed

Crusty bread, for serving (optional)

White Bean Cassoulet with Pork & Lentils

ACTIVE TIME 20 min. | **TOTAL TIME** 6 hr. 25 min. or 8 hr. 25 min. | **SERVES** 4

1. Place the bacon on a paper towel–lined plate and microwave on high until crisp, about 4 minutes. Cut into 1-inch pieces.

2. In a 5- to 6-quart slow cooker, whisk together the chicken broth, wine and tomato paste. Add the tomatoes, onion and garlic and mix to combine. Fold in the pork butt, bacon and thyme. Cook, covered, until the pork easily pulls apart, 5 to 6 hours on high or 7 to 8 hours on low.

3. Thirty-five minutes before serving, discard the thyme, then gently stir in the lentils. With slow cooker on high, cover and continue cooking until the lentils are just tender, 30 to 35 minutes. Gently fold in the beans and cook until heated through, about 3 minutes. Serve with crusty bread if desired.

PER SERVING *About 465 calories, 13 g fat (4 g saturated fat), 46 g protein, 775 mg sodium, 44 g carbohydrates, 13 g fiber*

1 15-ounce can tomato sauce

1 tablespoon chopped chipotle chile in
adobo plus 1 tablespoon sauce

½ teaspoon ground cumin

Kosher salt

1 onion, thinly sliced

2 garlic cloves, chopped

1 pound flank steak, cut crosswise into
2-inch-thick strips

1 15-ounce can black beans, rinsed

4 large tortillas, warmed

1 cup shredded extra-sharp
Cheddar cheese

2 cups shredded lettuce

1 cup chopped fresh cilantro

1 cup pico de gallo

Sour cream, sliced jalapeño and lime
wedges, for serving (optional)

◄ Smoky Shredded Beef Burritos

ACTIVE TIME 20 min. | **TOTAL TIME** 4 hr. 20 min. or 7 hr. 20 min. | **SERVES** 4

1. In a 5- to 6-quart slow cooker, whisk together the tomato sauce, chipotles and adobo, cumin and ½ teaspoon salt; stir in the onion and garlic.

2. Nestle the beef into the tomato-onion mixture and cook, covered, until it shreds easily, 4 to 5 hours on high or 7 to 8 hours on low.

3. Transfer the beef to a bowl. Spoon off and discard any fat in the slow cooker. Add the beans to the slow cooker; cook on high until heated through, 3 minutes. Using two forks, shred the beef, then toss with the beans.

4. Fill the tortillas with the beef mixture, Cheddar, lettuce, cilantro and pico de gallo, and roll them up. Serve with sour cream, jalapeño and lime wedges if desired.

PER SERVING *About 615 calories, 24 g fat (11 g saturated fat), 40 g protein, 2,015 mg sodium, 65 g carbohydrates, 10 g fiber*

¼ cup miso

¼ cup soy sauce

3 tablespoons gochujang (Korean hot
pepper paste) or sriracha, plus more
for serving

1 tablespoon sesame oil

1 teaspoon pepper

1 boneless pork shoulder (about
4 pounds), trimmed of excess fat
and quartered

Lettuce leaves and sliced radishes,
cucumbers and scallions,
for serving

Gochujang Pork Lettuce Wraps

ACTIVE TIME 10 min. | **TOTAL TIME** 6 hr. 10 min. | **SERVES** 8

1. In a small bowl, whisk together the miso, soy sauce, gochujang, sesame oil and pepper. Combine the pork with soy mixture and marinate in refrigerator overnight if desired. Add the pork and marinade to a 5- to 6-quart slow cooker, cover and cook until the pork is tender, 6 to 7 hours on high or 8 to 10 hours on low.

2. Shred the pork and serve with lettuce leaves, radishes, cucumbers, scallions and additional gochujang or sriracha.

PER SERVING *(PORK ONLY) About 450 calories, 21 g fat (7 g saturated fat), 53 g protein, 784 mg sodium, 6 g carbohydrates, 1 g fiber*

TIP To make this in the Instant Pot instead, cook the pork and soy mixture on high pressure for 1 hour. Then follow the directions outlined in step 2.

1 13½-ounce can light coconut milk

1½ tablespoons vegetable bouillon base (we used Better Than Bouillon)

3 tablespoons grated peeled fresh ginger, divided

1 tablespoon curry powder

1 tablespoon turmeric

½ teaspoon cardamom

Kosher salt

1½ cups yellow lentils, rinsed and picked over

1 15-ounce can diced tomatoes

2 pounds butternut squash, peeled, seeded, and cut into ½-inch pieces (about 4 cups)

1 medium onion, chopped

¼ cup olive oil

2 large scallions, thinly sliced

1 teaspoon grated lemon zest, plus 2 tablespoons lemon juice (from 1 lemon)

Cooked rice and plain yogurt, for serving (optional)

Curried Butternut Squash Stew

ACTIVE TIME 20 min. | **TOTAL TIME** 5 hr. 30 min. or 7 hr. | **SERVES** 4

1. In a 5- to 6-quart slow cooker, whisk together the coconut milk, vegetable bouillon base, 1 tablespoon of the ginger, the curry powder, turmeric, cardamom, 4 cups water and 1 teaspoon salt.

2. Add the lentils, tomatoes (and their juice), squash and onion and stir to combine. Cook, covered, until most of the liquid has been absorbed and lentils are tender, 6 to 7 hours on low or 4½ to 5 hours on high.

3. In a small bowl, whisk together the olive oil, scallions, lemon zest and juice, remaining 2 tablespoons ginger and ¼ teaspoon salt.

4. Serve the stew with rice and a dollop of yogurt if desired. Drizzle with the lemon-scallion oil.

PER SERVING *About 582 calories, 21.5 g fat (8 g saturated fat), 21 g protein, 1,552 mg sodium, 80 g carbohydrates, 24 g fiber*

TIP Keep this recipe quick and easy by using precooked rice.

2 carrots, cut into 3-inch pieces

1 onion, cut into wedges

¼ cup sweet red cherry peppers, finely chopped

1 1-inch piece fresh ginger, peeled and thinly sliced

4 garlic cloves, chopped

1 14½-ounce can diced tomatoes, drained

½ cup dry white wine

6 pounds boneless lamb shoulder, trimmed and cut into 2-inch pieces

Kosher salt and pepper

1 15-ounce can white beans, rinsed

Chopped fresh flat-leaf parsley, for topping

Crusty bread, for serving (optional)

Lamb & White Bean Stew

ACTIVE TIME 20 min. | **TOTAL TIME** 5 hr. 20 min. or 8 hr. 20 min. | **SERVES** 4

1. In a 5- to 6-quart slow cooker, combine the carrots, onion, cherry peppers, ginger, garlic, tomatoes and wine.

2. Season the lamb with ¼ teaspoon each salt and pepper, add it to the slow cooker, and toss to combine. Cook, covered, until the lamb is cooked through and easily pulls apart, 6 to 8 hours on low or 4 to 5 hours on high.

3. Add the beans to the slow cooker and cook until heated through, about 3 minutes. Sprinkle with the parsley and serve with bread if desired.

PER SERVING *About 524 calories, 17 g fat (6 g saturated fat), 56 g protein, 1,157 mg sodium, 35 g carbohydrates, 7 g fiber*

TIP For Moroccan flavor, swap the white beans for chickpeas and add 1 teaspoon ground cumin before cooking.

12 ounces beer

1 tablespoon low-sodium chicken bouillon base (we used Better Than Bouillon)

2 teaspoons ground cumin

Kosher salt and pepper

1½ pounds boneless, skinless chicken thighs, trimmed

12 ounces tomatillos, cut into ½-inch pieces

4 cloves garlic, finely chopped

1 onion, finely chopped

1 poblano, cut into ¼-inch pieces

½ small bunch cilantro, plus leaves for serving

1 28-ounce can hominy, rinsed

¼ cup fresh lime juice

Diced avocado and sliced radishes, for serving

◂ Chicken Pozole Verde

ACTIVE TIME 30 min. | **TOTAL TIME** 4 hr. 15 min. or 6 hr. to 7 hr. | **SERVES** 4–6

1. In 5- to 6-quart slow cooker, combine the beer, bouillon base, cumin, 2 cups water and ½ teaspoon each salt and pepper.

2. Add the chicken, tomatillos, garlic, onion, poblano and cilantro and mix to combine. Cook, covered, until chicken is easily pulled apart, 4 to 5 hours on high or 6 to 7 hours on low.

3. Remove and discard the cilantro from the slow cooker; then, using 2 forks, break chicken into smaller pieces. Add hominy and cook, covered, until tender, 3 to 4 minutes. Stir in the lime juice and serve with cilantro, avocado and radishes if desired.

PER SERVING *About 320 calories, 8 g fat (2 g saturated fat), 31 g protein, 819 mg sodium, 27 g carbohydrates, 7g fiber*

4 slices smoked bacon

1 14½-ounce can petite diced tomatoes

2 tablespoons Dijon mustard

Kosher salt and pepper

1½ cups green split peas

2 medium carrots, sliced

2 stalks celery, sliced

1 large onion, diced

4 garlic cloves, minced

6 thyme sprigs

Croutons, crisp bacon and chopped fresh flat-leaf parsley, for serving (optional)

Split Pea & Tomato Soup with Bacon

ACTIVE TIME 15 min. | **TOTAL TIME** 5 hr. 15 min. or 8 hr. 15 min. | **SERVES** 4

1. Microwave the bacon slices on high for 3 minutes.

2. Meanwhile, in a 5- to 6-quart slow cooker, combine the tomatoes (including their juice), mustard, 5 cups water and ½ teaspoon each salt and pepper.

3. Add the partially cooked bacon to the slow cooker along with the split peas, carrots, celery, onion, garlic and thyme and stir to combine. Cook, covered, until the vegetables are tender and the peas have broken down, 7 to 8 hours on low or 4 to 5 hours on high.

4. Remove and discard the bacon and thyme. Divide among bowls and top with croutons, bacon and parsley if desired.

PER SERVING *About 300 calories, 2.5 g fat (1 g saturated fat), 17 g protein, 704 mg sodium, 54 g carbohydrates, 19 g fiber*

TIP Make this soup ahead and freeze it in individual portions to always have something tasty and filling on hand.

Recipe Index

::::::::::::::::::::::::::

Index

::::::::::::::::::::::::::

Photo Credits

::::::::::::::::::::::::::

Font & Back Cover Photography: Mike Garten

Spine: Getty© Maksym Rudoi

Photography: Mike Garten (1, 2, 4, 6, 8, 15, 16, 19, 20, 22, 28, 30, 32, 36, 40, 42, 44, 48, 54, 56, 58, 64, 66, 68, 69, 70, 72, 74, 76, 78, 80, 84, 86, 88, 92, 94, 101, 102, 104, 106, 110, 112, 116, 118, 124, 134, 136, 140, 144, 148, 150, 156, 158, 162, 166, 168, 170, 172, 175, 176, 178, 182, 184, 186, 188, 190, 192, 194, 196, 198, 202, 208, 210, 232, 240, 244, 256); Danielle Daly (11, 26, 34, 60, 62, 82, 114, 122, 152, 154, 160, 180, 214, 238); ©Steve Giralt (13, 130, 224, 228); ©Con Poulos (38, 90, 120, 126, 206, 216, 220, 226, 236); ©Hector Sanchez (96, 132); ©Becky Luigart-Stayner (108); Emily Kate Roemer (164); ©Christopher Testani (204); ©Romulo Yanes (213, 234); ©Brian Woodcock (218); ©Chris Court (222); ©Marcus Nilsson (230); ©Ryan Dausch (242)

HEARST
HOME

Cover and book design by Ashley Prine,
Tandem Books

Library of Congress Cataloging-in-Publication
Data Available on request

10 9 8 7 6 5 4 3 2 1

Published by Hearst Home, an imprint of
Hearst Books/Hearst Communications, Inc.
300 W 57th Street
New York, NY 10019

Good Housekeeping, Hearst Home, the Hearst
Home logo, and Hearst Books are registered
trademarks of Hearst Communications, Inc.

For information about custom
editions, special sales, premium
and corporate purchases:
hearst.com/magazines/hearst-books

Printed in United States of America

ISBN 978-1-950785-79-7